GW00705950

Dear Children's Book

I am delighted to be writing to you
CHILDREN'S BOOKS: A Parent's Guide.
talking to parents, teachers, librarians and children's authors to find out
how to make it easier to choose the right book for the right child.

With the sheer number of children's books available finding books can be an
overwhelming experience. As a parent, I appreciate guidance when choosing
books. The Parent's Guide enables you to select by age range, subject or
author as well as providing suggestions for reluctant and gifted readers.
This information all helps parents to feel confident about book choices.

This year we are particularly proud of our new association with the
Pre-school Learning Alliance. This is the largest association providing care and
education for under fives. Look out for the picture books that are endorsed
by The Alliance as being particularly suitable for pre-school children.

The Parent's Guide provides something for everybody and we feel sure
that you will find it invaluable.

P. J. Milnes-Smith

Philippa Milnes-Smith
Publisher, Penguin Children's Books

PUFFIN BOOKS

PUBLISHED BY THE PENGUIN GROUP

Penguin Books Ltd, 27 Wrights Lane, London W8 5TZ, England

Penguin Books USA Inc, 375 Hudson Street, New York, New York 10014, USA

Penguin Books Australia Ltd, Ringwood, Victoria, Australia

Penguin Books Canada Ltd, 10 Alcorn Avenue, Toronto, Ontario, Canada, M4V 3B2

Penguin Books (NZ) Ltd, 182–190 Wairau Road, Auckland 10, New Zealand

Penguin Books Ltd, Registered Offices: Harmondsworth, Middlesex, England

First published 1995

Second Edition 1996

Text copyright © Puffin Books, 1995

All rights reserved

Printed by Yale Press Limited, Norwood, London SE25 5LY

Designed by Ross Advertising and Design Ltd, Chesham, Bucks, HP5 1PG

CONTENTS

HOW TO USE THIS GUIDE

AGE RANGES

The guide is divided into age ranges to allow quick and easy access. Use age as a starting point, but don't discount books outside your child's age range, as age does not always reflect reading ability or interest level.

SUBJECT

Does your child have a particular interest? For example, if your child is mad about trains, look in the subject index for the books about trains.

AUTHORS

The author index lists the books featured in this guide as well as other books written by this author for the same interest level.

RELUCTANT READER

If you are looking for books for reluctant readers look at the reluctant reader section within their age range. Also look for books with the icon within that age range and the age range below.

GIFTED READER

If you are looking for books for gifted readers look at the gifted reader section within their age range. Also look for books with the icon within that age range and the age range above.

KEY

A handy key gives further information about each title such as **award winners** and **reluctant reader** choices.

 AWARD-WINNING BOOK

 AWARD-WINNING AUTHOR

 A BOOK IN A SERIES

 RELUCTANT READERS

 GIFTED READERS

 TV OR FILM

 COLOUR ILLUSTRATIONS

 BLACK AND WHITE ILLUSTRATIONS

 PUFFIN MODERN CLASSIC EDITION ALSO AVAILABLE

 ENDORSED BY THE PRE-SCHOOL LEARNING ALLIANCE

NB. All of the books contained in this Guide are suitable for the National Curriculum England and Wales.

FIRST BOOKS FOR BABIES AND TODDLERS

'A child is never too young for books. Holding back on books until a child can read is like not talking to her until she can speak'

Dr Penelope Leach, leading childcare expert

All parents want to prepare their children for life in the best way possible. As a parent, you teach a variety of essential skills including walking, feeding, talking and READING.

SHARED READING IS VITAL

Making books a part of your children's lives is all about starting early. Babies as young as six months old enjoy being read to. Although you may feel silly at first, you don't have to be an expert — just take a deep breath and have a go. Remember that when you read to your children, you are teaching them the basic mechanics of turning a page, holding a book the right way up and looking at the words and pictures. These subtle messages are all part of the skill of reading.

Books are essential to develop their imaginations and expand their world. The PLAYTIME BOOKS series introduces children to new ideas and experiences in a lively and entertaining way. They are ideal for sharing as well as being excellent for encouraging imaginative play.

> **HINT:** Never force reading. If your child is fidgeting, give up and try again. READING SHOULD ALWAYS BE FUN.

NOT THAT ONE AGAIN!

The cry of many a harassed parent, but you will inevitably be asked to read the same story over and over again. It may be frustrating but this is exactly how children learn to read. Children will soon become familiar with the story and begin to memorise the words. They may even protest when you miss a line or skip a page! Eventually they will join in and read along with you, so encourage them to finish your sentences and to ask lots of questions.

FIRST BOOKS FOR BABIES AND TODDLERS

LEARNING THROUGH PLAY

Children learn most skills through practise and learning to read is no exception. To become an ACTIVE reader, children need to 'read' and play alone. Hopefully, they will turn pages and point to the pictures as well as put the books on their heads and build houses. Although you may end up with the odd soggy or ripped page, remember that flaps can be stuck back on and books dried out. What's more important is that your children discover that books are fun.

CHOOSING THE RIGHT BOOK

- Babies love books they can touch and play with — look for books with added interest such as flaps, peepholes and funny shapes.
- For very young babies choose large, colourful and simple pictures.
- Books with simple first words are a good starting point when learning to read.
- Look for books that feature things that are part of your children's lives, whether it's nappies, food or the pet cat.
- Children can relate to recognisable situations like going to playschool or taking a bath.
- Familiar characters — if your children love one particular SPOT book, rest assured they will love the rest of the books about this playful puppy.
- Find books that encourage them to develop their imaginations through new experiences and concepts.
- Rhyming, rhythmic language or lots of repetition all help children to predict what comes next.
- When looking for educational books, try ones that find exciting ways to introduce colours or numbers.

HINT: Reading stories to your children at bedtime is a great way to get reading into their daily routine.

SEE BACK OF GUIDE FOR MONEY-OFF
PICTURE PUFFIN BOOKS

NB. All books in this section are suitable for Key Stage 1 England and Wales National Curriculum.

FIRST BOOKS FOR BABIES

JANET AND ALLAN AHLBERG

THE BABY'S CATALOGUE

The world of babies in a nutshell. Beautiful, intricate illustrations make this a perfect book for sharing and talking about again and again.

'A book which guarantees hours of warm sharing and talking'
Books for Keeps

PEEPO!

Ideal book for babies to play with as they look through the peepholes and discover the story. With repetitive rhymes and a family theme, this book is a firm favourite.

'The best book ever published for babies'
Books for Your Children

DEAR ZOO
by Rod Campbell

The ingenious use of flaps and repetitive text invites babies to guess and then discover which animal has been sent from the zoo to a little boy looking for a pet.

NOISY FARM
by Rod Campbell

Discover by lifting the flaps which animal makes what noise – a racket of a read.

'Colourful, unfussy – it's just right'
Woman and Home

THE VERY HUNGRY CATERPILLAR BOARD BOOK
by Eric Carle

The chunky board format adds a new dimension to this classic picture book. Very young children can put their fingers through the holes and really play with this book without fear of ripping the pages.

ERIC HILL

WHERE'S SPOT?

Babies love surprises and SPOT delivers just that in Eric Hill's series of lift-the-flap books about this lovable puppy. Follow SPOT through all his adventures and mishaps.

'Beautifully simple, cleverly designed ...irresistible'
Child Education

NOAH AND THE RABBITS
by Sally Kilroy

Noah searches the ark for a place to put the rabbits and finds animals in the most unlikely places. It's fun, bright and great for memorising the animals under the flaps.

MY BOOK
by Ron Maris

This book allows you to unravel the simple storyline by opening the doors.

'A beautiful, almost wordless bedtime book which is a delight'
Parents Magazine

MOONLIGHT
by Jan Ormerod

The familiar bed time scene is told through pictures not words, allowing you to share the book and make up your own story.

CAT IN A FLAP
by Shoo Rayner

This contemporary picture flap book, with its original story and imaginative use of text, is a real cat and mouse tale readers can become actively involved in.

MUMMY WHERE ARE YOU?
by Harriet Ziefert

Very young children can lift the flaps to help Hippo in his search for his mummy.

BOOKS FOR TODDLERS

EACH PEACH PEAR PLUM
by Janet & Allan Ahlberg

A mixture of nursery characters and 'I-Spy' by the talented Ahlbergs. The combination of rhyming text and detailed illustrations encourages both language development and interaction.

'Deceptively simple. EACH PEACH PEAR PLUM is a work of a genius'
Elaine Moss

WHO SANK THE BOAT?
by Pamela Allen

Reader and child will have fun asking repeatedly *'Who Sank the Boat?'* as this hilarious tale unfolds.

RAYMOND BRIGGS

THE SNOWMAN
A children's classic and continual bestseller. Readers are encouraged to use their imagination to create the story around Raymond Briggs' amazing pictures. Also a major animated film.

'A book with no words! How on earth do I read that to my child? Worry not, for this story is so alive, so vibrant, you'll probably find that your child reads it to you!'
Practical Parenting

MR GUMPY'S OUTING
by John Burningham

When Mr Gumpy goes out in his boat, everybody he meets wants to come along too... with disastrous results. Simple, repetitive language that is easy to memorise and say together.

'Perfect... points out that squabbling spoils things, and as always John Burningham's illustrations are superb'
The Times

ERIC CARLE

THE VERY HUNGRY CATERPILLAR
The bright collage-style pictures and cut-out holes convey a simple story of growing up. 25 years on, the popularity of this munching caterpillar grows and grows, making it the best-selling picture book for this age group.

1,2,3 TO THE ZOO
Count the brightly coloured animals on the train as it trundles on it's way to the zoo. See if you can spot the cheeky little mouse that turns up in the most unexpected places.

HAIRY MACLARY FROM DONALDSON'S DAIRY
by Lynley Dodd

A rhyming, witty story, easy for even the youngest child to follow. Part of a best-selling series that follows the adventures of Hairy Maclary and his animal friends.

GOING TO PLAYSCHOOL
by Sarah Garland

Real life situations told through this series of brightly illustrated picture books. Ideal for introducing young children to new situations in a reassuring way.

'Sarah Garland's drawings are full of pleasing detail...'
The Observer

SPOT'S WALK IN THE WOODS
by Eric Hill

The large text is punctuated with small illustrated flaps. Use the picture to guess the word, then lift the flap. The guess and show element helps toddlers understand that text has meaning within a story.

LUCY & TOM'S ABC

A breakthrough in alphabet books. Traditional ABC words are incorporated within the text, providing a greater learning experience.

'A refreshingly new ABC learning formula'
The Guardian

ROSIE'S WALK
by Pat Hutchins

Rosie the hen takes a walk pursued by a cunning fox. Unwittingly, she leads him into one disaster after another but manages to return home safely.

'Very amusing and good value'
Practical Parenting

TITCH
by Pat Hutchins

Titch is the smallest in his family, and everything his brother and sister have seems bigger and better than anything Titch has. A great book for inspiring confidence in young children.

THIS LITTLE PUFFIN...
Edited by Elizabeth Matterson

A classic treasury of rhymes, songs and games for young children. The collection is the result of a two year research project and a further twenty years experience. The author has discovered children's favourites as well as those of the adults who sing with them.

HELEN NICOLL AND JAN PIEŃKOWSKI

MEG AND MOG

A vivid series of books about Meg the Witch and her cat Mog. Simple text integrated into vibrant pictures provides lots of fun.

'Strong, bright colours and simple, bold illustrations are as comic as the tale, and have children spellbound in no time at all'
Practical Parenting

DINOSAUR ROAR!
by Paul & Henrietta Stickland
NEW IN APRIL

These dinosaurs have one thing in common – they're all HUNGRY! The witty rhyming text and amazing monster-sized illustrations will appeal to every dinosaur lover.

MY CAT LIKES TO HIDE IN BOXES
by Eve Sutton & Lynley Dodd

Cats from around the world do strange and exotic things but...
'My cat likes to hide in boxes'.
This fun rhyming picture book gives clues to the beginner reader about what comes next.

THE ELEPHANT AND THE BAD BABY
by Elfrida Vipont & Raymond Briggs

A classic picture book, beautifully illustrated by Raymond Briggs. Repetitive text with a simple message – always say 'please'!

PLAYTIME BOOKS

Lively and entertaining, Playtime Books are perfect to share with your pre-school children. Excellent for encouraging imaginative play and introducing new words and concepts.

MAX AND THE MAGIC WORD
by Colin & Jacqui Hawkins

Everyone knows the magic word except Max. A fun way to learn about manners and especially good for reading aloud, lots of scope for different voices.

I'M GOING ON A DRAGON HUNT
by Maurice Jones & Charlotte Firmin

A young explorer goes for a walk that turns into an adventure. The repetitive text helps you to predict how he will cope with the obstacles he encounters.

DAISY THINKS SHE IS A BABY
by Lisa Kopper

This book will make your toddler chuckle. Daisy is a dog, that thinks she is a baby but the real baby doesn't like that.

ANDREW'S BATH
by David McPhail

Andrew hates baths! But when his parents let him take a bath on his own, suddenly bathtime becomes a terrific adventure. A book that even the dirtiest of young children will be unable to resist!

TEN LITTLE TEDDY BEARS
by Maureen Roffey

Rhyming text and lively illustrations give children a fun introduction to numbers and counting.

CHECKLIST – BOOKS FOR BABIES & TODDLERS

For your convenience we have put together the list of books featured in this section of the guide. All titles are available from bookshops. Please note prices are subject to change and some titles may become temporarily unavailable. Remember to check the author index for more books by the same author.

FIRST BOOKS FOR BABIES

THE BABY'S CATALOGUE
Janet & Allan Ahlberg
0140503854 £4.99

PEEPO! *Janet & Allan Ahlberg*
0140503846 £4.99

DEAR ZOO *Rod Campbell*
014050446X £4.99

NOISY FARM *Rod Campbell*
0140502939 £4.50

THE VERY HUNGRY CATERPILLAR BOARD BOOK
Eric Carle
0241003008 £4.50

WHERE'S SPOT? *Eric Hill*
0140504206 £4.99

NOAH AND THE RABBITS
Sally Kilroy
0140543465 £4.99

MY BOOK *Ron Maris*
0140505237 £4.50

MOONLIGHT *Jan Ormerod*
0140503722 £4.50

CAT IN A FLAP *Shoo Rayner*
0140548602 £3.99

MUMMY WHERE ARE YOU?
Harriet Ziefert
0140508996 £3.99

BOOKS FOR TODDLERS

EACH PEACH PEAR PLUM
Janet & Allan Ahlberg
0140509194 £4.99

WHO SANK THE BOAT?
Pamela Allen
0140509402 £4.50

THE SNOWMAN *Raymond Briggs*
0140503501 £4.99

MR GUMPY'S OUTING
John Burningham
0140502548 £4.99

THE VERY HUNGRY CATERPILLAR
Eric Carle
0140500871 £4.50

1,2,3 TO THE ZOO *Eric Carle*
0140509267 £4.50

HAIRY MACLARY FROM DONALDSON'S DAIRY
Lynley Dodd
0140505318 £4.50

GOING TO PLAYSCHOOL
Sarah Garland
0140553630 £3.99

SPOT'S WALK IN THE WOODS
Eric Hill
014055274X £4.50

LUCY AND TOM'S ABC
Shirley Hughes
0140505210 £4.99

ROSIE'S WALK *Pat Hutchins*
0140500324 £4.50

TITCH *Pat Hutchins*
0140500960 £4.99

THIS LITTLE PUFFIN...
Elizabeth Matterson (Ed)
0140340483 £5.50

MEG AND MOG
Helen Nicoll & Jan Pieńkowski
0140501177 £3.99

*DINOSAUR ROAR!
Paul and Henrietta Stickland
0140557024 £4.99

MY CAT LIKES TO HIDE IN BOXES
Eve Sutton & Lynley Dodd
0140502424 £3.99

THE ELEPHANT & THE BAD BABY
Elfrida Vipont & Raymond Briggs
0140500480 £4.99

* Available from April 1996

PLAYTIME BOOKS

MAX AND THE MAGIC WORD
Colin & Jacqui Hawkins
0140553606 £4.50

I'M GOING ON A DRAGON HUNT
Maurice Jones & Charlotte Firmin
0140553908 £4.50

DAISY THINKS SHE IS A BABY
Lisa Kopper
0140548262 £4.50

ANDREW'S BATH
David McPhail
0140507485 £3.99

TEN LITTLE TEDDY BEARS
Maureen Roffey
0140545786 £3.99

SEE BACK OF PARENT'S GUIDE FOR PICTURE PUFFIN MONEY-OFF VOUCHER

Notes

HINT: If you are unable to find a book in your local bookshop, ask them to order it using the ISBN number.

PICTURE BOOKS 4 YEARS +

Learning to read is a gradual process and all children will learn at their own pace. But of course there is plenty you can do to encourage them.

READING CLUES

As your children's reading confidence grows, don't stop reading to them! Now is the key time to help them to decipher all the clues on the page that help to tell the story. These clues may be words or pictures, so talk about the illustrations and ask them questions about the story as it develops. What do they think is going to happen next? Which words can they recognise on the page? This interaction will help them to work out the new words on the page and to understand the meaning of the story rather than JUST the words. You may find that children will begin by reading you the story using the pictures alone. Even if this bears no resemblance to the real story, give them lots of feedback as they are showing an understanding of how a story works.

YOUR CHILDREN READING TO YOU

Always praise your children's efforts and don't put pressure on them to read to you. They will gladly read when they are ready. Learning to read depends on confidence and security; your children will want to return to familiar, much-loved books that you may feel are too 'easy' for them. This is all part of the learning process, and building confidence is essential so that they can move on. Once they have gained reading confidence, watch out for PUFFIN PICTURE STORY BOOKS. These books are ideal for readers who need satisfying stories in a familiar picture book format. They are also wonderful to read aloud to younger children.

HINT: Run your finger along under the words when you are reading to your children — they will then understand that the symbols are important.

PICTURE BOOKS 4 YEARS +

SUSTAINING INTEREST

Allow your children to experience as many books as possible. Make good use of your local library and encourage them to explore new formats and a wide range of stories. This will all help to instil a love of reading.

CHOOSING THE RIGHT BOOK

- Look for substantial picture books with longer text and more sophisticated stories.
- Detailed illustrations give you more to talk about.
- Address day-to-day issues that worry your children through the safety of books.
- Look for books that match the INTEREST level of your child.
- Read other books by an author you've enjoyed.
- Make friends with picture book characters, who will show your children new experiences in a familiar way.
- Characters are useful when teaching your children to recognise colours, numbers and words.
- Books that use text in imaginative ways can make reading fun. Look out for speech bubbles, labels and words under flaps.

HINT: Look for vocabulary that you know your children are using; print size is less important.

SEE BACK OF GUIDE FOR MONEY-OFF PICTURE PUFFIN BOOKS

PICTURE BOOKS 4 YEARS +

NB. All books in this section are suitable for Key Stage 1 England and Wales National Curriculum

STARTING SCHOOL
by Janet & Allan Ahlberg

The book in which children can find out exactly what going to school entails. A must for calming anxieties and firing enthusiasm in all pre-school children.

'I can't think of a better book to pop into every five-year-old's satchel'
Parents

BEAR HUNT
by Anthony Browne

Bear ingeniously escapes from two hunters, with the use of his magic pencil. Children will love the way bear draws himself out of tricky situations.

THE BAD-TEMPERED LADYBIRD
Eric Carle

The Bad-Tempered Ladybird thinks it is bigger and better than anyone else! But being bad-tempered doesn't get him anywhere and he soon learns to share.

SOMETHING ELSE
by Kathryn Cave & Chris Riddell

A sensitive tale of tolerance and belonging, with quirky, loveable characters.

'It is poignant, funny and original'
The Sunday Times

BABETTE COLE

WINNI ALLFOURS

Horse-mad children will adore this wacky book about a girl who turns into a horse after eating lots of carrots.

'Her stories engage both adults and children in a deliciously subversive complicity'
The Mail on Sunday

DINOSAURS AND ALL THAT RUBBISH

by *Michael Foreman*

An environmental message conveyed through the story of ever popular dinosaurs having to clean up the mess created by humans.

WILFRED GORDON MCDONALD PARTRIDGE

by *Mem Fox & Julie Vivas*

Wilfred discovers that his friend Miss Nancy has lost her memory. He is determined to find it for her but first he must discover what memories are.

THE BAKED BEAN QUEEN

by *Rose Impey & Sue Porter*

The Baked Bean Queen loves baked beans so much that she eats them for breakfast, lunch and dinner. The perfect book for any children who know exactly what they want!

GRANNY'S QUILT

by *Penny Ives*

Granny's life story is told through the pieces of fabric from her many different dresses sown together in a patchwork quilt.

'Captivating...Nostalgic, gentle and comforting'
Independent on Sunday

THE BEAST WITH A THOUSAND TEETH

by *Terry Jones & Michael Foreman*

In a far-off city lived a fearsome beast who terrorized the citizens. But one day, Sam the baker's son discovered that as well as having a taste for human beings, the monster was also very fond of fairy cakes. An hilarious fairy tale with magical illustrations.

NICE WORK, LITTLE WOLF!

by Hilda Offen

When Little Wolf lands in their cucumber frame, the Porkers set him to work straight away. But their little slave begins to grow, and one day they push him just that tiny bit too far!

LONG NECK AND THUNDER FOOT

Helen Piers & Michael Foreman

A dinosaur story that teaches us all not to judge people on first impressions.

BEATRIX POTTER

THE TALE OF PETER RABBIT

This book and Potter's other classic tales deserve a place on all children's bookcases. This is an ideal first introduction, in a large format with clear, readable print.

THE BUNK-BED BUS

by Frank Rodgers

You're never too old to learn as Sam and Janet's Granny demonstrates by winning the local art competition with her bunk-bed bus.

MOVING

by Michael Rosen & Sophy Williams

A rhyming picture book that gently addresses the issues of moving house from the point-of-view of the family cat.

FRED

by Posy Simmonds

Nick and Sophie's lazy cat Fred
has died and they really miss him.
Then one night they are woken by a
loud **MEEYOW** and venturing
into the garden they discover
from the other neighbourhood
cats that Fred was no ordinary cat.
A touching look at loss for the
very young, told partly in
comic–strip format.

'*...enchanting – an instant classic*'
The Sunday Telegraph

GLASSES WHO NEEDS 'EM

by Lane Smith
NEW IN MAY

"*I can't wear glasses*" says the young
patient. "*Only dorks wear glasses.*" The
mad optician points out a little-known
world of glasses wearers. Seeing is
believing in this hilarious world of the
unexpected. Ideal for anyone who
doesn't want to wear glasses.

GOING WEST

by Martin Waddell &
Philippe Dupasquier

This picture book follows the
adventures of a pioneering family on
a dangerous and difficult journey
across America to find a new home.
The panoramic illustrations bring real
life and vitality to this touching story.

THE SELFISH GIANT

Oscar Wilde & Michael Foreman & Freire Wright

Oscar Wilde's gentle fairy tale about
friendship and sharing is a moving
bedtime read.

THE DO-IT-YOURSELF HOUSE
THAT JACK BUILT

by John Yeoman & Quentin Blake

An original retelling of this popular
nursery rhyme combined with
hilariously intricate illustrations,
make this a gloriously funny book to
share.

PUFFIN PICTURE STORY BOOKS

Puffin Picture Story Books combine satisfying stories with superb illustrations.
While they are ideal for readers who still need the interest that colour illustrations provide,
they are also perfect for reading aloud to younger children.

BEWARE OF BOYS
by Tony Blundell

A clever little boy manages to
outwit a very hungry wolf in
no ordinary fairy tale.
Hilarious slapstick fun as the boy
decides the wolf needs a special
cookery lesson.

THE PATCHWORK QUILT
*by Valerie Flournoy
& Jerry Pinkney*

One year in the life of a family is
lovingly reflected in the colourful
patchwork quilt that Grandma
makes. A touching story that
celebrates families.

'This is a "happy family" story'
Reading Time

THE GREAT WHITE
MAN-EATING SHARK
Margaret Mahy & Jonathan Allen

Nervine is a very good actor, but
rather plain. In fact, he looks
very like a shark, and more than
anything he loves to shoot
through the water. But his
cunning plan to clear the
water at Caramel Cove
badly misfires. A funny,
cautionary tale.

SPIDER THE HORRIBLE CAT
*by Nanette Newman
& Michael Foreman*

An ideal story to read at bedtime
about Spider a bad-tempered, boss-
eyed, snarly cat who lives with a
sweet old lady.

LITTLE RED RIDING HOOD
Retold by Tony Ross

There's a wolf, and a grandmother,
and a little girl in a red cape, of
course but Tony Ross' version of
this well-known story is very
different from the traditional
fairy tale!

CAPTAIN PUGWASH
by John Ryan

Captain Pugwash was the bravest, most handsome pirate on the seven seas – or so he liked to think! Beginner readers can follow this character into the Young Puffin series.

THE RASCALLY CAKE
by Jeanne Willis & Korky Paul

An hilarious story, told in rhyme, of Skumskins O'Parsley who decides to bake a cake with more revolting ingredients than you can possibly imagine. When the cake tries to eat him, he knows it is time to mend his ghastly ways.

NON-FICTION

SPOT'S BIG BOOK OF COLOURS, SHAPES AND NUMBERS

by Eric Hill

Spot will introduce young children to colours, shapes and numbers in this big, bold book that they will understand and enjoy.

© Eric Hill 1994

SPOT'S BIG BOOK OF WORDS
by Eric Hill

Who better to help your children to read than Spot? The vibrant illustrations bring a wide range of words to life.

PUFFIN FIRST PICTURE DICTIONARY

by Brian Thompson & Celia Berridge

A simple picture dictionary that familiarizes children with the alphabet and helps them to learn how to use a dictionary.

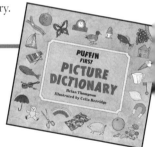

CHECKLIST – PICTURE BOOKS FOR 4 YEARS +

For your convenience we have put together the list of books featured in this section of the guide. All titles are available from bookshops. Please note prices are subject to change and some titles may become temporarily unavailable. Remember to check the author index for more books by the same author.

STARTING SCHOOL
Janet & Allan Ahlberg
014050737X   £4.99

BEAR HUNT *Anthony Browne*
0140553568   £4.50

THE BAD-TEMPERED LADYBIRD
Eric Carle
0140503986   £4.99

SOMETHING ELSE
Kathryn Cave & Chris Riddell
0140549072   £4.99

WINNI ALLFOURS *Babette Cole*
014054917X   £4.99

DINOSAURS AND ALL THAT RUBBISH
Michael Foreman
014055260X   £4.99

WILFRED GORDON MCDONALD PARTRIDGE
Mem Fox & Julie Vivas
0140505865   £4.50

THE BAKED BEAN QUEEN
Rose Impey & Sue Porter
0140507019   £3.99

GRANNY'S QUILT *Penny Ives*
0140545603   £4.99

THE BEAST WITH A THOUSAND TEETH
Terry Jones & Michael Foreman
0140552553   £3.99

NICE WORK, LITTLE WOLF!
Hilda Offen
0140544127   £4.99

LONG NECK AND THUNDER FOOT
Helen Piers & Michael Foreman
0140504192   £4.99

THE TALE OF PETER RABBIT
Beatrix Potter
0140542957   £3.99

THE BUNK-BED BUS *Frank Rodgers*
014050849X   £3.99

MOVING
Michael Rosen & Sophy Williams
0140548955   £4.99

FRED *Posy Simmonds*
0140509658   £3.99

*GLASSES WHO NEEDS 'EM
Lane Smith
0140556524   £4.99

GOING WEST
Martin Waddell &
Philippe Dupasquier
0140504737   £4.50

THE SELFISH GIANT
Oscar Wilde, Michael Foreman
& Freire Wright
0140503838   £3.99

THE DO-IT-YOURSELF HOUSE THAT JACK BUILT
John Yeoman & Quentin Blake
0140553231   £4.99

* Available from May 1996

PUFFIN PICTURE STORY BOOKS

BEWARE OF BOYS *Tony Blundell*
014054156X £4.99

THE PATCHWORK QUILT
Valerie Flournoy & Jerry Pinkney
0140554335 £4.99

**THE GREAT WHITE
MAN-EATING SHARK**
*Margaret Mahy &
Jonathan Allen*
0140554246 £4.99

SPIDER THE HORRIBLE CAT
*Nanette Newman &
Michael Foreman*
014054898X £4.99

LITTLE RED RIDING HOOD
Retold by Tony Ross
014055436X £3.99

CAPTAIN PUGWASH *John Ryan*
014055453X £4.99

THE RASCALLY CAKE
Jeanne Willis & Korky Paul
0140554726 £4.99

NON-FICTION

SPOT'S BIG BOOK OF WORDS
Eric Hill
0140548998 £4.99

**SPOT'S BIG BOOK OF COLOURS,
SHAPES & NUMBERS**
Eric Hill
0140555145 £4.99

PUFFIN FIRST PICTURE DICTIONARY
Brian Thompson & Celia Berridge
0140507779 £4.25

SEE BACK OF PARENT'S GUIDE FOR PICTURE PUFFIN MONEY-OFF VOUCHER

Notes

HINT: If you are unable to find a book in your local bookshop, ask them to order it using the ISBN number.

EARLY READERS 6 YEARS +

Although your children will now be learning to read at school, it is more important than ever to encourage reading at home. If you have exposed them to books, they may already recognise words and understand how stories work; they may even be reading.

Your children's teachers may use a variety of ways to teach reading, including reading schemes, book-making, book weeks and author visits. Your input at this time is still vital to further your children's reading development. By providing them with different books at home, you will broaden their experience and enjoyment. At this stage, your children will also be having their first taste of the National Curriculum (for details about the National Curriculum see page 75.)

PICTURE BOOKS FOR BEGINNER READERS

Picture Books can be enjoyed at any age. The picture books in this section have been selected because they combine a more challenging, lengthy text with the added security and enjoyment of wonderful, full colour illustrations.

AFTER PICTURE BOOKS WHAT NEXT?

Pictures are still important and early reading books should have pictures and text on each page. Look for series that combine exciting illustrations with interesting stories in just this way. If your children enjoy one book in the series, give them more until they feel confident to move on.

CHOOSING THE RIGHT BOOK

- Look for plenty of interesting illustrations and clear print.
- Look at the vocabulary of a book to assess the interest level.
- Try to find a subject that interests your children.
- If your children enjoy books by particular authors, keep a note of the names and look for more books by those authors.
- Short stories or chapters provide manageable chunks of reading.
- Balance interesting stories that copy real life with ones that stretch even the most vivid imagination.
- Children will enjoy reading pages that use text in an unusual way eg. speech bubbles.

HINT: Look out for Happy Families, Ready, Steady, Read! and First Young Puffins which are ideal for beginner readers.

EARLY READERS 6 YEARS +

YOUNG PUFFINS

Children's interest in books will grow as their reading skills develop. Their initial appetite for reading should be fed and fattened with a variety of books! With over 300 Young Puffins, there is something to appeal to all children's interests and abilities.

DEVELOPING READERS – look for Young Puffin Read Alones with short chapters or stories, simple words and sentences and lots of illustrations. These are for readers who are gaining confidence.

CONFIDENT READERS – look out for Young Puffin Story Books with longer more developed stories or chapters, simple sentences and pictures throughout. This series is for children who have mastered the basic skills of reading.

POETRY

At this stage children will still gain a lot of pleasure from the richness and rhythm of language. Poetry books are enjoyable, often hilarious and easy to dip in and out of.

RELUCTANT READERS

If your children are showing signs of being unwilling to read, don't despair. Either find books around a subject they are intensely interested in, or look for books that are simple and that will guarantee reading success. A sense of achievement is important to combat a reluctant attitude. Non-fiction with short chunks of text, illustrations and straight forward language is ideal for reluctant readers.

GIFTED READERS

Children who read fluently and confidently need to be exposed to a wide range of reading material. It is essential to find books that satisfy their growing appetite as readers while also reflecting their emotional maturity.

NB. All books in this section are suitable for Key Stage 1 England and Wales National Curriculum

PICTURE BOOKS

IT WAS A DARK AND STORMY NIGHT

Janet & Allan Ahlberg

"It was a dark and stormy night..." the classic opening for a classic Ahlberg picture book, packed with action and storytelling adventure. Antonio, a small boy who has been kidnapped by brigands, passes the night in their cave weaving incredible stories about their own exploits. Through his cleverly constructed story he manages to escape.

THE MINPINS

by Roald Dahl & Patrick Benson

'Dahl is in sparkling form...
The Minpins *has brought out in Benson a new lyrical quality'*
The Times Literary Supplement

THE ENORMOUS CROCODILE

by Roald Dahl & Quentin Blake

The enormous crocodile decides he wants to eat a child for lunch, but all the animals in the jungle manage to foil his plans. A great book for reading aloud.

REVOLTING RHYMES

by Roald Dahl & Quentin Blake

Six of the best known nursery tales retold with some extremely surprising twists from the blood curdling Dahl.

'Pure pleasure. Raucous, irreverent, inventive'
The Times Literary Supplement

THE TRUE STORY OF THE 3 LITTLE PIGS!

by Jon Scieszka & Lane Smith

An hilarious, inventive retelling of the popular fairy tale by the Big Bad Wolf.

'Children of an age to understand irony will respond to its wit and inventiveness...'
The Sunday Times

BROTHER EAGLE, SISTER SKY

by Chief Seattle & Susan Jeffers

This is a powerful plea for conservation to which every child and every adult will respond.

'His words are simple and effective. They moved me and I think they will move children as well. Susan Jeffers' excellent illustrations will help to hold their attention'
The Daily Telegraph

Allan Ahlberg's

HAPPY FAMILIES

A classic series that is perfect for bridging the gap between picture books and early reading books. The master storyteller, Allan Ahlberg, is joined by a variety of top illustrators to produce miniature masterpieces. The series allows early readers the freedom to explore the whole series at their own pace.

'If ever a series was designed to lighten the darkness of parents and children worried about reading, this is it' **Books For Your Children**

MRS WOBBLE THE WAITRESS
by Janet & Allan Ahlberg

The one thing you don't want to do as a waitress is WOBBLE. When Mrs Wobble is sacked for dropping food on the customers, she decides to open her own cafe. With the help of the juggling waiters, her new cafe is a huge success.

MASTER BUN THE BAKERS' BOY
by Allan Ahlberg & Fritz Wegner

Bertie Bun is browned off with being the Baker's boy. He swaps jobs with the Butcher's and Barber's boys but eventually uses his loaf and decides that bread is not so bad after all.

COMING SOON!

Look out for two new Happy Families' books available from September 1996.

SEE BACK OF GUIDE FOR MONEY-OFF VOUCHER.

MISS DIRT THE DUSTMAN'S DAUGHTER
by Allan Ahlberg & Tony Ross

MRS VOLE THE VET
by Allan Ahlberg & Emma Chichester Clark

ready, steady, read!

New readers love to read proper books with characters who have real adventures. This is just what Ready, Steady, Read! offers them, as well as good, clear print and illustrations on every page that give clues to the text. The lively vocabulary will help children to discover the joys of reading. All titles are by established and well-known authors and illustrators.

'The Ready, Steady, Read! series has a welcoming look and feel'
The Times Educational Supplement

HEDGEHOGS DON'T EAT HAMBURGERS
by Vivian French & Chris Fisher

Hector and Hattie and Harry and Hester set off to find a nice juicy hamburger, but Fox and Badger want four nice juicy hedgehogs for their tea. Two funny stories about four friendly hedgehogs.

SWIM, SAM, SWIM
by Leon Rosselson & Anthony Lewis

Sam is a young frog who wants to play not swim. When he invents a new game he surprises everyone by how well he can swim.

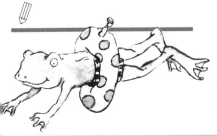

First Young Puffin

Lively, easy-to-read stories with colour illustrations on every page. These are ideal for children who are starting to read on their own as they feel like real books with spines.

BELLA AT THE BALLET
by Brian Ball
& Hilda Offen

Bella is annoyed that her baby brother has to come to her first ballet class. She thinks he's a pest but realises that he's just having fun too. It's a great story for beginner ballerinas and anyone who has an annoying little brother!

DUMPLING
by Dick King-Smith & Jo Davies

Dumpling the Dachshund wants to be long and sausage-shaped, not short and plump. But when her wish is granted by a witch's cat, she becomes the longest dog ever!

SEE BACK OF GUIDE FOR MONEY-OFF VOUCHER

DEVELOPING READERS

Short stories or chapters, simple words and sentences, pictures throughout.

ONE NIL
by Tony Bradman

Football mad? Dave Brown is! This football story will get them just as hooked on reading as they are on football.

A GIFT FROM WINKLESEA
by Helen Cresswell

Dan and his sister, Mary, find a present for their mother at the seaside. The egg-shaped stone sits proudly on the mantelpiece until it hatches into a strange sea creature and plenty of fun ensues.

'A good, simple story well told'
Venue

ROALD DAHL

Books by Roald Dahl for the developing reader that are sure to inspire them to keep on reading.

THE MAGIC FINGER
Illustrated by Tony Ross

Have you ever wanted to stop something that seems terribly cruel? One little girl has the power to do just that with a magic finger that can flash punishment at people that make her angry. Full of delightful Dahl magic with a strong environmental theme.

STRANGER DANGER
by Anne Fine

Joe has learnt his safety rules about strangers, but he gets confused about what a 'stranger' is and how he can still be polite if he's not allowed to talk to them. With one amusing blunder after another, Joe discovers that a little common sense comes in handy!

THE SHRINKING OF TREEHORN
by *Florence Parry Heide*

A story to make all grown-ups sit up and take notice! Children love this hilarious tale in which Treehorn has to find his own way out of trouble when the adults refuse to believe him. Great for building confidence.

IT'S TOO FRIGHTENING FOR ME!
by *Shirley Hughes*

This is no namby-pamby story, but a first deliciously creepy venture into exciting grown-up stories. Ideal for those readers who feel old and bold enough to endure their first adventure story – without the scary ending.

THE TWIG THING
by *Jan Mark*

When Ella, Rosie and their dad move into a new house it has lot's of windows and stairs but no garden. This is a warm story about readjusting to new surroundings.

DUSTBIN CHARLIE
by *Ann Pilling*

Timothy Charles Treadwell's very best thing is to watch the rubbish men with their yellow lorries. Even the contents of an old skip hold exciting treasures for him.

ROSA'S SINGING GRANDFATHER
by *Leon Rosselson*

These warm and sensitive stories follow the lives of an over-worked mum, her daughter Rosa and Rosa's grandfather. He has a song for every occasion – even one to stop Rosa being afraid of the dark.

'The clarity and optimism of this book should make it very welcoming to new independent readers'
Books for Keeps

CAPTAIN PUGWASH AND THE MIDNIGHT FEAST
by *John Ryan*

Shiver me timbers – join the jolliest of pirates, Captain Pugwash, as he bumbles through two amusing adventures.

CONFIDENT READERS

Longer, more developed stories or chapters, simple sentences, pictures throughout.

COMPUTER FOR CHARLIE
by Joy Allen

Charlie is blamed for erasing an important program on his dad's new computer and his chance to go to summer camp looks in jeopardy! A story about one boy's passion for football and computers.

THE RAILWAY CAT
by Phyllis Arkle

Alfie the railway cat is a favourite with everybody, except the new porter, Hack. He has a plan to get rid of Alfie, but will it work?

ADVENTURE ON SKULL ISLAND
by Tony Bradman

Pirates are always a popular choice with children. This story about a pirate family, *the Bluebeards*, who set sail in their ship, the *Saucy Sally*, is equally popular with boys and girls.

THE GHOST AT NO. 13
by Gyles Brandreth

One of a series starring Hamlet Brown, who lives at No. 13 Irving Terrace. In this story he finds that he has something his sister, Susan, doesn't – a rather unusual friend!

MR MAJEIKA
by Humphrey Carpenter

In the first book in this popular series we meet Mr Majeika – the school teacher with a magical difference.

FANTASTIC MR FOX
By Roald Dahl

Mr Fox is so brainy he out-foxes his enemies, the mean and nasty farmers Boggis, Bunce and Bean.

DICK KING-SMITH

GEORGE SPEAKS

The hilarious account of George, the extraordinary baby who learns to speak at the early age of FOUR WEEKS.

THE HODGEHEG

Crossing the road is a dangerous business for hedgehogs and Max has got a lot to learn before he can reach the park; but when he finds a solution to the traffic problem Max becomes a hero. A funny and salutary tale about road safety.

SEE BACK OF GUIDE FOR MONEY-OFF VOUCHER

THE GREAT PIRATICAL RUMBUSTIFICATION

by Margaret Mahy
Illustrated by Quentin Blake

Two hilarious stories with very short chapters for pirate fans and anyone who enjoys a hearty YO HO HO of a read. Quentin Blake's illustrations bring the whole set of amazing events to life.

THE WORST WITCH

Mildred Hubble is the worst witch at Miss Cackle's Academy and disaster strikes when she crashes her broomstick. A satisfying read for any child facing difficulties at school. Look out for other Worst Witch titles.

CLEVER POLLY AND THE STUPID WOLF

by Catherine Storr

The first amusing tale about a clever little girl called Polly who, in a series of humorous adventures, outwits a rather stupid wolf.

THE GO-AHEAD GANG

by Robert Swindells

The Go-Ahead Gang got together in the forties when there were no TVs, videos and computers. They played cops and robbers, tin can squat and tig. They spent a lot of time looking for things to do and some of the things they did led them into trouble.

KING KEITH AND THE JOLLY LODGER

by Kaye Umansky

A right royal romp! The royal family has run out of gold and times are hard. Queen Freda decides they should take in a lodger. When the pirate Captain Roger Jolly arrives everyone loves him except King Keith. He sets out to get rid of him and the fun begins.

GOBBOLINO THE WITCH'S CAT

by Ursula Moray Williams

The first adventure of Gobbolino, a well-loved character who, unlike his mother and sister, isn't cut out to be a witch's cat.

FEATHERBRAINS

by John Yeoman
& Quentin Blake

When two battery hens are accidently released from their cage they don't know what to make of the world beyond. Luckily a kindly jackdaw takes them under his wing, but the hens are slow learners and sometimes even he can't keep them out of trouble!

Story collections particularly good for reading aloud to children aged 5 to 8 years old.

AGE RANGED STORY COLLECTIONS
Edited by Sara and Stephen Corrin

A series of stories that have been put together to make choosing books for children easy. These comprehensive collections of superb tales have been carefully graded to suit the developing interests and imaginations of the different age groups. Nine books covering the under-fives to tens-and-over. These are perfect stories for adults and children to share.

THE YOUNG PUFFIN BOOK OF BEDTIME STORIES
Edited by Barbara Ireson

From classic tales of princes and dragons, to modern stories of schools and supermarkets, these irresistible collections of stories are ideal for you to read aloud at bedtime. Sweet dreams guaranteed!

MEET MY FRIENDS
Edited by Kaye Webb

This is a great introduction to many of the best-loved characters of children's fiction, including Mrs Pepperpot, Teddy Robinson, Captain Pugwash and Fantastic Mr Fox. Carefully chosen extracts give children a taste of some remarkable stories.

PLEASE MRS BUTLER
by Allan Ahlberg
Illustrated by Fritz Wegner

Celebrating its tenth anniversary, this is a children's classic from well-known writer and ex-teacher Allan Ahlberg. This collection of poems takes a funny and realistic look at classroom life.

EARLY IN THE MORNING
by Charles Causley
Illustrated by Michael Foreman

From the award-winning poet Charles Causley, this collection offers a blend of originality and traditionalism. Illustrated by renowned artist Michael Foreman.

POEMS FOR 7-YEAR-OLDS-AND-UNDER
Edited by Helen Nicoll

Poetry from a diverse range of favourite writers, including Roald Dahl, Robert Louis Stevenson, Robert Frost and Roger McGough.

NON-FICTION

PUFFIN FACTFINDERS

A bright new introduction to reference books. Large text integrated with full-colour illustrations make the facts accessible to young non-fiction readers. Clearly marked chapters and easy-to-use contents and index that cover a range of unusual subjects.

BALLET AND DANCE *by Maggie Tucker*

FANTASTIC SEA CREATURES *by Rupert Matthews*

INVENTIONS *by Chris Oxlade*

MONSTER ANIMALS *by Gerald Legg*

NATURAL DISASTERS *by Carol Watson*

WARRIORS *by Rupert Matthews*

THE WORST WITCH SPELLING BOOK

by Jill Murphy & Rose Griffiths

Make spells not spelling mistakes! Join the Worst Witch in wizard word games, spooky spelling puzzles and crafty crosswords all of "witch" will make spelling easy and fun.

THE YEAR I WAS BORN

Compiled by Sally Tagholm

A day-by-day picture of the year your child was born. Lots of illustrations, facts, figures and information that are both amusing and useful. Children and adults will love dipping into these books.

RELUCTANT READERS

THE HA HA BONK BOOK
by Janet & Allan Ahlberg

A book full of jokes to tell dads, mums, baby brothers, teachers and just about anybody else you think of!

FATHER CHRISTMAS
by Raymond Briggs

If daunted by large blocks of text, reluctant readers may find the comic strip format more accessible. Father Christmas is so funny it is a great read at any time of year.

PASS IT POLLY
by Sarah Garland

An unusual football story with big text, speech bubbles and lively dialogue.

FRED
by Posy Simmonds

A cleverly designed picture book, almost completely told using speech bubbles. A touching story that older children will find rewarding.

'This book is a winner'
The Times Educational Supplement

THE DO-IT-YOURSELF HOUSE THAT JACK BUILT
by John Yeoman & Quentin Blake

A familiar rhyme told in a lunatic fashion with funny illustrations and hilarious comments.

GIFTED READERS

FAIRY TALES
by Terry Jones & Michael Foreman

Ideal for children who are familiar with the fairy tale format. The combination of fantasy, magic and Michael Foreman's exquisite illustrations will stretch the imagination of the gifted reader.

THERE'S A VIKING IN MY BED
by Jeremy Strong

Sigurd the Viking finds himself in the twentieth century. This funny story encourages the reader to compare contrasting lives in the past and present.

NO HICKORY, NO DICKORY, NO DOCK
by John Agard & Grace Nichols

A celebration of Caribbean sound and rhythm brought together in a collection of chants, songs and rhyme. Language to savour.

CHECKLIST – BOOKS FOR CHILDREN 6 YEARS +

For your convenience we have put together the list of books featured in this section of the guide. All titles are available from bookshops. Please note prices are subject to change and some titles may become temporarily unavailable. Remember to check the author index for more books by the same author.

PICTURE BOOKS

IT WAS A DARK AND STORMY NIGHT
Janet & Allan Ahlberg
0140545867 £5.99

THE MINPINS
Roald Dahl & Patrick Benson
0140543716 £5.99

THE ENORMOUS CROCODILE
Roald Dahl & Quentin Blake
0140503420 £4.99

ROALD DAHL'S REVOLTING RHYMES
Roald Dahl & Quentin Blake
0140504230 £4.99

THE TRUE STORY OF THE 3 LITTLE PIGS
Jon Scieszka & Lane Smith
0140540563 £4.50

BROTHER EAGLE, SISTER SKY
Chief Seattle & Susan Jeffers
014054514X £5.99

BEGINNER READERS

HAPPY FAMILIES

See back of Parent's Guide for
Happy Families money-off voucher.

MASTER BUN THE BAKERS' BOY
Allan Ahlberg & Fritz Wegner
0140323449 £3.25

MRS WOBBLE THE WAITRESS
Janet & Allan Ahlberg
0140312390 £3.50

MISS DIRT THE DUSTMAN'S DAUGHTER*
Allan Ahlberg & Tony Ross
0140378820 £3.50

MRS VOLE THE VET*
Allan Ahlberg &
Emma Chichester Clark
0140378804 £3.50

* Available from September

READY, STEADY, READ!

HEDGEHOGS DON'T EAT HAMBURGERS
Vivian French & Chris Fisher
0140364099 £3.50

SWIM, SAM, SWIM
Leon Rosselson & Anthony Lewis
0140365524 £3.50

FIRST YOUNG PUFFINS

See back of Parent's Guide for
First Young Puffins money-off voucher.

BELLA AT THE BALLET
Brian Ball & Hilda Offen
0140375244 £3.50

DUMPLING
Dick King-Smith & Jo Davies
0140373748 £3.50

DEVELOPING READERS

ONE NIL *Tony Bradman*
0140319832 £3.25

A GIFT FROM WINKLESEA
Helen Cresswell
0140304932 £3.25

THE MAGIC FINGER *Roald Dahl*
0140341625 £3.99

STRANGER DANGER *Anne Fine*
0140343024 £3.25

THE SHRINKING OF TREEHORN
Florence Parry Heide
014030746X £3.25

IT'S TOO FRIGHTENING FOR ME!
Shirley Hughes
0140320083 £3.50

THE TWIG THING *Jan Mark*
0140326413 £3.25

DUSTBIN CHARLIE *Ann Pilling*
0140323910 £3.25

ROSA'S SINGING GRANDFATHER
Leon Rosselson
0140345876 £3.50

CAPTAIN PUGWASH AND THE MIDNIGHT FEAST *John Ryan*
0140319239 £3.25

CONFIDENT READERS

COMPUTER FOR CHARLIE *Joy Allen*
0140340580 £3.50

THE RAILWAY CAT
Phyllis Arkle
0140345159 £4.99

ADVENTURE ON SKULL ISLAND
Tony Bradman
014034070X £2.99

THE GHOST AT NO.13
Gyles Brandreth
0140319840 £3.25

MR MAJEIKA *Humphrey Carpenter*
0140316779 £3.50

FANTASTIC MR FOX *Roald Dahl*
0140326715 £3.50

GEORGE SPEAKS *Dick King-Smith*
014032397X £3.50

THE HODGEHEG *Dick King-Smith*
0140325034 £3.50

See back of Parent's Guide for
Dick King-Smith money-off voucher.

**THE GREAT PIRATICAL
RUMBUSTIFICATION** *Margaret Mahy*
0140312617 £3.25

THE WORST WITCH *Jill Murphy*
0140311084 £3.50

CLEVER POLLY AND THE STUPID WOLF
Catherine Storr
0140364633 £3.50

THE GO-AHEAD GANG
Robert Swindells
0140365079 £3.50

KING KEITH AND THE JOLLY LODGER
Kaye Umansky
0140345191 £3.25

GOBBOLINO THE WITCH'S CAT
Ursula Moray Williams
0140302395 £3.99

FEATHERBRAINS
John Yeoman & Quentin Blake
0140362967 £2.99

STORY COLLECTIONS

Sara & Stephen Corrin (Ed)
STORIES FOR UNDER FIVES
0140311009 £3.50

MORE STORIES FOR UNDER FIVES
0140325298 £3.50

STORIES FOR FIVE YEAR OLDS
0140308393 £3.99

STORIES FOR SIX YEAR OLDS
0140307850 £4.50

STORIES FOR SEVEN YEAR OLDS
0140308822 £3.99

Barbara Ireson (Ed)
**THE FIRST YOUNG PUFFIN BOOK OF
BEDTIME STORIES**
0140368094 £3.99

**THE SECOND YOUNG PUFFIN BOOK OF
BEDTIME STORIES**
0140368116 £3.50

**THE THIRD YOUNG PUFFIN BOOK OF
BEDTIME STORIES**
0140370196 £3.50

**THE FOURTH YOUNG PUFFIN BOOK OF
BEDTIME STORIES**
014037020X £3.99

MEET MY FRIENDS *Kay Webb*
0140342168 £3.99

POETRY

PLEASE MRS BUTLER *Allan Ahlberg*
0140314946 £3.99

EARLY IN THE MORNING
Charles Causley
0140320334 £3.25

POEMS FOR 7-YEAR-OLDS-AND-UNDER
Helen Nicoll (Ed)
014031489X £3.99

NON-FICTION

FACTFINDERS

BALLET & DANCE *Maggie Tucker*
0140376194 £3.99

FANTASTIC SEA CREATURES
Rupert Matthews
0140374086 £4.50

INVENTIONS *Chris Oxlade*
0140370854 £4.50

NATURAL DISASTERS *Carol Watson*
014037406X £4.50

WARRIORS *Rupert Matthews*
0140369511 £4.50

THE YEAR I WAS BORN 1988
Sally Tagholm
0140901159 £4.99

THE YEAR I WAS BORN 1989
Sally Tagholm
0140374019 £4.99

THE YEAR I WAS BORN 1990
Sally Tagholm
0140380639 £4.99

THE WORST WITCH SPELLING BOOK
Jill Murphy & Rose Griffiths
0140376720 £2.99

RELUCTANT READERS

THE HA HA BONK BOOK
Janet & Allan Ahlberg
0140314121 £3.50

FATHER CHRISTMAS *Raymond Briggs*
0140501258 £4.99

PASS IT POLLY *Sarah Garland*
0140555218 £3.99

FRED *Posy Simmonds*
0140509658 £3.99

**THE DO-IT-YOURSELF HOUSE THAT
JACK BUILT**
John Yeoman & Quentin Blake
0140553231 £4.99

GIFTED READERS

FAIRY TALES
Terry Jones & Michael Foreman
0140316426 £9.99

THERE'S A VIKING IN MY BED
Jeremy Strong
0140348786 £3.50

NO HICKORY, NO DICKORY, NO DOCK
John Agard & Grace Nichols
0140340270 £3.50

8 YEARS +

At this age children are very engrossed in school. The demands on their time are ever increasing with TV, computer games, hobbies, sport and friends uppermost in their priorities.

Many parents worry if their children are reading books or magazines that aren't seen as educational, but reading must also be about relaxing and reading purely for pleasure. We would soon tire of reading if we were put on a diet of classics and were never allowed to look at a newspaper or magazine; children thrive on variety too.

DEVELOPING UNDERSTANDING

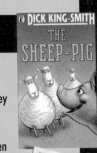

Most children in this age group are becoming more fluent readers who begin to develop a greater understanding of the content and meaning of stories. By reading about the experiences of others in fiction books or biographies, they start to discover a new way of looking at the world. Their growing sense of awareness and insight makes reading a more rewarding experience.

Many of the authors who write for this age group will be familiar to children as they may have enjoyed their books at a younger age. Children who are exposed to good quality writing early on will generally find it easier to express themselves.

STORY TIME IS STILL OK!

Older children still enjoy being read to. It's a good excuse to spend time together doing something relaxing. It also means you can read them books that seem too long for them to manage. There is nothing more exciting than a cliff-hanging bedtime story.

CHOOSING THE RIGHT BOOK

- Street cred is increasingly important, so find books that look good. Many children (especially boys) are very sensitive to books that they consider to be too 'babyish' or biased to one gender.

- Look for humourous books — it's the age of endless joke-telling and a fun way to get hooked.

- Books that address issues that are relevant to your children's growing awarenesss of the outside world.

- Poetry can be funny, rude or thought provoking.

- Computer and adventure gamebooks may be the answer for the game-playing maniac.

- Try to find books that will interest children. Look for books about favourite films or TV programmes.

- Non-fiction may be the only way to get non-readers interested, if the subject is one of their passions.

RELUCTANT READERS

Reading can be seen as just a school activity and children may feel that since they know how to read, there is no need to practise. But just as with playing the piano or football, they need to keep their skills fresh. Here are some simple guidelines to try to encourage the more reluctant reader to pick up a book.

- Be positive about reading.
- Books should be accessible and not strictly educational; try short stories or comic strip formats.
- Never force reading; the more you push, the more determined children might be not to read.
- Allow children to choose their own books and respect their decisions.
- Encourage children to talk about the books they are reading and show them that their interpretations and views on books are important.
- Read to children; you may just find something that turns them on and encourages them to read for themselves. They also gain much from watching a good reader in action.
- Don't forget picture books. Reluctant readers can use the text and the pictures to construct meaning.

GIFTED READERS

"Gifted readers should be stretched like elastic – carefully, so as not to lose the bounce." Jenny Green, author of Stretching the Gifted Reader Booklist (available from Puffin, see back of guide).

If a reader has mastered the skills of reading they will appreciate books that force them to become involved as well as books that demand a response. Gifted readers tend to be highly perceptive with the ability to empathise with the characters within a story. Books that explore differing emotions and strong characterisation specifically delight gifted readers.

HINT: If your children are enjoying a particular book at school, follow this up by looking for books by the same author.

NB. All books in this section are suitable for Key Stage 2 England and Wales National Curriculum

WOOF!

by Allan Ahlberg

When Eric turns into a dog he's quite rightly amazed! A very accessible read.

A NECKLACE OF RAINDROPS AND OTHER STORIES

by Joan Aiken
Illustrated by Jan Pieńkowski

Eight magical tales from around the world, with simple language and brilliant illustrations.

'What a marvellous writer Joan Aiken is. She provides more sheer enjoyment than anyone else I can think of'
The Guardian

CHILLERS

A series of thrillers, ghost stories and mysteries. If your children pick one up they won't want to put it down until the very last sentence. The text is presented in imaginative ways with lots of full page illustrations.

THE MIDNIGHT FOX

by Betsy Byars

Guaranteed to keep your children gripped, this is the exciting story of a boy's battle to save a wild fox. Humorous, moving and filled with suspense, this book appeals to both boys and girls.

ROALD DAHL

Full of humour, Roald Dahl's books have immense child appeal. The heroes and heroines are always children and they often make adults look silly. Dahl speaks to children at their own level and by doing so has become one of the world's most popular authors.

THE BFG

Sophie is snitched by a giant! Luckily for her it was no ordinary bone-crunching giant. Instead she is whisked off to giant land by the BFG, who is far too nice and jumbly to guzzle her up.

'You don't know what you've missed if you haven't read this one'
The Daily Telegraph

GEORGE'S MARVELLOUS MEDICINE

George's grandmother is as grumpy as a camel without a hump. When he can't stand this cantankerous old woman any more, he decides to cure her nastiness once and for all.

JAMES AND THE GIANT PEACH

James' aunts make his life a misery but something peculiar happens and he is taken on the most amazing and unbelievable journey.

THE WITCHES

No pointy hats and broomsticks here! This is a book about 'real witches' the ones that absolutely loathe children and are always plotting to get rid of them. Find out all you need to know to protect yourself from the most grotesque gang imaginable!

'Funny, wise and deliciously disgusting. A real book for children'
Whitbread Award Judges

THE PUFFIN BOOK OF TWENTIETH-CENTURY CHILDREN'S STORIES

Edited by Judith Elkin

Short extracts from some of the best-known authors of this century, might be just the thing to persuade children to go onto read the whole book. Judith Elkin has chosen exciting extracts, often with cliff-hanger endings, and all are great stories in themselves.

SEASONS OF SPLENDOUR

by Madhur Jaffrey
Illustrated by Michael Foreman

Ideal for reluctant readers as reading each short story gives a sense of achievement. Tales, myths and legends from India written by Madhur Jaffrey that draw on her own childhood experiences.

'Beautifully told...Madhur Jaffrey brings to [the stories] the freshness of the spoken word'
Woman and Home

THE SAGA OF ERIK THE VIKING

by Terry Jones
Illustrated by Michael Foreman

Each chapter begins a new adventure, so this book is easy to dip in and out of. The stories are simple to read and the subject matter is appealing and exciting. Particularly good for children who like adventure.

DICK KING-SMITH

LADY DAISY

Told with wit and humour, this is the story of a boy who dares to be different by his friendship with an extraordinary doll. Ideal for any child who has ever been bullied at school, the book also gives a fascinating insight into Victorian history.

THE SHEEP-PIG

Excitement and suspense are combined with warmth, humour and appealing illustrations to produce an adventure animal lovers will find impossible to resist! BABE the film is based on this story by Dick King-Smith.

'Brilliantly funny'
The Daily Telegraph

See back of Guide for money-off voucher

STIG OF THE DUMP

by Clive King

An adventure between a young boy, Barney, and Stig, a caveman who lives in a rubbish dump. This story, based around an unusual friendship, shows the differences between Barney's life and that of a caveman.

THE BORROWERS

by Mary Norton

This classic tale of the tiny family has strong imaginative appeal – as well as providing children with the perfect excuse as to the whereabouts of mislaid belongings! Ideal for chidren who enjoy fantasies set in the real world.

'This is fantasy at its best'
Books for Keeps

MRS FRISBY AND THE RATS OF NIMH

by Robert C O'Brien

Mrs Frisby's adventures with the Rats of Nimh – rats made super–intelligent through a series of biological experiments – will appeal to animal lovers and science fantasy enthusiasts alike.

PHILIP RIDLEY

Illustrated by Chris Riddell

'I try to maintain the pace of a film or computer game...'
Philip Ridley

KASPER IN THE GLITTER

A fantastical story of a young boy who finds himself in danger when he tries to make his mother happy. A thought provoking but accessible look at homelessness.

METEORITE SPOON

Filly and Fergal escape from the war-zone of their parents' volatile marriage into a parallel world of equally precarious love.

SEE BACK OF GUIDE FOR MONEY-OFF VOUCHER

THE TIME WARP TRIO: THE GOOD THE BAD AND THE GOOFY

by Jon Scieszka
Illustrated by Lane Smith

An action-packed, riotously funny adventure story, told in short, simple sentences with cartoon-style illustrations.

THE KARATE PRINCESS

by Jeremy Strong

This is a fairy tale with a twist – and a few kicks, punches and well-aimed blows to boot.

PONGWIFFY

by Kaye Umansky

Pongwiffy is the smelliest, ugliest witch you are ever likely to bump into and, accompanied by Hugo, the fearless hamster from Amsterdam, she causes hilarious havoc amongst the witches of Witchway Wood.

'...this will appeal to the delicious anarchy in children'
Prima

I LIKE THIS STORY

Edited by Kaye Webb

A taste of fifty favourite stories which leaves you longing for more!

CHARLOTTE'S WEB

by E B White

The enduringly popular story of how Charlotte, the beautiful and intelligent grey spider, saves Wilbur the pig from the usual nasty fate of plump pigs! This will appeal to all animal enthusiasts and also provides a gentle introduction to the subject of death.

POETRY

LAUGHTER IS AN EGG

by John Agard

The poems in this book are contemporary, short and immediate. The message is clear...laughter won't go away! Caribbean poet John Agard's energy lifts off the page with every word.

'He shows just how much laughter there is in poetry – his style matches the subject matter perfectly, whether the form is a rap or a ballad'

Children's Books of the Year

ROGER McGOUGH

SKY IN THE PIE

Roger McGough has many intriguing poems for his readers to taste: some to choke with laughter on, some to chew very slowly. His use of the pun, twist and punchline and his perceptive look at life destroy the idea that poetry is 'pretentious', in his hands it's nothing if not accessible.

'The hit of the year...his ability to make us smile and be sad at the same time is McGough's great gift'

Signal

THE PUFFIN BOOK OF TWENTIETH-CENTURY CHILDREN'S VERSE

Edited by Brian Patten
Illustrated by Michael Foreman

Exciting and often unexpected poems sit alongside some of the twentieth century's best-loved classics.

QUICK, LET'S GET OUT OF HERE!

by Michael Rosen
Illustrated by Quentin Blake

Zany poems about everyday things that you do, say, know and think. Thought-provoking, for older more experienced poetry readers.

'Rosen has hit the jackpot'
Anne Harvey

HOT DOG AND OTHER POEMS

by Kit Wright
Illustrated by Posy Simmonds

Witty rhymes about everyday subjects like tidying your bedroom, with characters like Dave Dirt, who is adept at throwing up. Kit Wright's poems are fast moving and good for maintaining children's interest through humour.

COMPUTER GAMEBOOKS

Part novel – part game, these books allow readers to control their own destiny.
They need to be ready for the challenges with all their wits and skills about them.
Ideal for your very own gamesmaster!

SONIC THE HEDGEHOG

Help the Hedgehog with attitude as he tries to outwit the dreaded and deranged inventor Robotnik. Six series titles to play. Sonic is SEGA'S top character.

LEMMINGS

Lemmings is available on more formats than any other computer game and sales have made it the number one game of all time. The reader takes an amazing trip through all the Lemmings' worlds, in which only the bravest and cleverest survive.

NON-FICTION

THE NUTTY FOOTY BOOK

by Martin Chatterton

Do you know someone who is nuts about football? Whether a player or a supporter, they will love the nutty facts, trivia, jokes and puzzles in this book.

WAR GAME

by Michael Foreman

Michael Foreman captures the empathy that grew between the two armies suffering during the First World War.

'Superb piece of story-telling'
Daily Express

WAR BOY

by Michael Foreman

When a fire bomb exploded in his bedroom in Lowestoft, young Michael Foreman knew that he and his family were living on the front line. A child's-eye view of the war for children, their parents and their grandparents to share.

THE MIDNIGHT FEAST JOKE BOOK

by Shoo Rayner

Tuck into this scrummy selection of jokes. Then close the book and when the lights go out, see how the cover glows!

THE YEAR I WAS BORN

Compiled by Sally Tagholm

A day-by-day picture of the year your child was born. Lots of illustrations, facts, figures and information that are both amusing and useful. Children and adults will love dipping into these books.

100 QUESTIONS AND ANSWERS: AGE 7+

100 of the most often asked questions answered in these comprehensive, large format information books. The questions are organised by theme: for example, Why do stars twinkle?

FILM AND TV
by Neil Cook & Kay Barnham

DANGEROUS AND DEADLY
by Rupert Matthews

DINOSAURS AND OTHER PREHISTORIC ANIMALS
by John Cooper

EXPLORERS
by Margarette Lincoln

FOOTBALL
by Neil Cook & Paul Harrison

PLANET EARTH
by Roger Coote

PONIES AND HORSES
by Jenny Millington

SPACE AND SPACEFLIGHT
by Harry Ford & Kay Barnham

CRIME AND PUNISHMENT
by Anita Ganeri

TOMMY NINER AND THE PLANET OF DANGER

by Tony Bradman

A fast-paced zooming space adventure with short chapters. Guaranteed to help even the most reluctant reader take off with reading.

FUNGUS THE BOGEYMAN

by Raymond Briggs

Children will pick this one every time as Fungus is so totally disgusting! Snot to be missed!

'You need a strong stomach and a quick eye'
The Sunday Times

THE STINKY CHEESE MAN AND OTHER FAIRLY STUPID TALES

by Jon Scieszka & Lane Smith

'Off the wall fairy stories...made even more anarchic by creatively used typography and lusciously surreal illustrations.'
Independent on Sunday

STANLEY BAGSHAW AND THE TWENTY TWO TON WHALE

by Bob Wilson

The Stanley Bagshaw books have many layers of humour. The comic strip format is accessible and ideal for sustaining interest.

THE BEAR NOBODY WANTED

by Janet & Allan Ahlberg

Before the lonely teddy bear can find someone to make him feel wanted he must learn some hard lessons about being proud and selfish.

THE KINGDOM UNDER THE SEA

by Joan Aiken & Jan Pieńkowski

Eleven hauntingly beautiful stories from Eastern Europe retold by a magical storyteller. Dramatically illustrated in a silhouette style by Jan Pieńkowski.

THIS POEM DOESN'T RHYME

by Gerard Benson (Ed)

An award-winning collection that demonstrates that poems can have rhythm, structure and meaning without having to rhyme.

UNDER THE HAWTHORN TREE

by Marita Conlon-McKenna

High quality historical fiction about the struggle to survive during the potato famine in Ireland.

'Not only historically true but fictionally vivid, and the relationships are tender and moving'
The Sunday Times

CHECKLIST – BOOKS FOR CHILDREN 8 YEARS +

For your convenience we have put together the list of books featured in this section of the guide. All titles are available from bookshops. Please note prices are subject to change and some titles may become temporarily unavailable. Remember to check the author index for more books by the same author.

WOOF! *Allan Ahlberg*
0140319964 £3.99

A NECKLACE OF RAINDROPS AND OTHER STORIES *Joan Aiken*
014036613X £3.99

THE MIDNIGHT FOX *Betsy Byars*
014030844X £3.50

CHILLERS

THE DAY MATT SOLD GREAT GRANDMA
Eleanor Allen & Jane Cope
0140364315 £3.50

CLIVE AND THE MISSING FINGER
Sarah Garland
0140364285 £3.50

JIMMY WOODS AND THE BIG BAD WOLF
Mick Gowar & Barry Wilkinson
0140364293 £3.50

THE REAL PORKY PHILIPS
Mark Haddon
0140364307 £2.99

THE BFG
Roald Dahl & Quentin Blake
0140315977 £4.99

GEORGE'S MARVELLOUS MEDICINE
Roald Dahl & Quentin Blake
014031492X £3.99

JAMES & THE GIANT PEACH
Roald Dahl & Quentin Blake
0140371567 £4.99

THE WITCHES
Roald Dahl & Quentin Blake
0140317309 £4.99

THE PUFFIN BOOK OF TWENTIETH-CENTURY CHILDREN'S STORIES *Judith Elkin (Ed)*
0140325492 £6.99

SEASONS OF SPLENDOUR
Madhur Jaffrey
0140346996 £4.99

THE SAGA OF ERIK THE VIKING
Terry Jones & Michael Foreman
0140322612 £4.99

STIG OF THE DUMP *Clive King*
0140301968 £3.99

LADY DAISY *Dick King-Smith*
0140344160 £3.99

THE SHEEP-PIG *Dick King-Smith*
0140318399 £3.50

See back of Parent's Guide for money-off Dick King-Smith books.

THE BORROWERS *Mary Norton*
0140301100 £3.99

MRS FRISBY AND THE RATS OF NIMH
Robert C O'Brien
0140366148 £4.99

KASPER IN THE GLITTER *Philip Ridley*
0140368914 £4.50

METEORITE SPOON *Philip Ridley*
0140368906 £3.99

See back of Parent's Guide for money-off Philip Ridley books.

THE TIME WARP TRIO: THE GOOD, THE BAD AND THE GOOFY
Jon Scieszka
0140363998 £3.25

THE KARATE PRINCESS
Jeremy Strong
0140328041 £3.50

PONGWIFFY *Kaye Umansky*
0140342214 £3.99

I LIKE THIS STORY *Kaye Webb*
0140320008 £4.99

CHARLOTTE'S WEB *E B White*
0140301852 £3.99

POETRY

LAUGHTER IS AN EGG *John Agard*
0140340726 £3.50

SKY IN THE PIE *Roger McGough*
0140316124 £3.50

THE PUFFIN BOOK OF TWENTIETH-CENTURY CHILDREN'S VERSE *Brian Patten*
0140322361 £6.99

QUICK, LET'S GET OUT OF HERE!
Michael Rosen
0140317848 £3.99

HOT DOG AND OTHER POEMS *Kit Wright*
0140313362   £2.99

SONIC THE HEDGEHOG 1 *James Wallis*
0140376291   £3.99

SONIC THE HEDGEHOG 2 *James Wallis*
0140376305   £3.99

SONIC THE HEDGEHOG 3
Nigel Gross & Jon Sutherland
0140376313   £3.99

SONIC THE HEDGEHOG 4
Nigel Gross & Jon Sutherland
0140376321   £3.99

SONIC THE HEDGEHOG 5
Marc Gascoigne & Jonathon Green
0140378472   £3.99

SONIC THE HEDGEHOG 6
Marc Gascoigne & Jonathon Green
0140378480   £3.99

LEMMINGS 1: THE GENESIS QUEST
Nigel Gross & Jon Sutherland
0140373519   £3.99

LEMMINGS 2: THE HYPNOSIS ENIGMA
Nigel Gross & Jon Sutherland
0140373527   £3.99

NON-FICTION

THE NUTTY FOOTY BOOK
Martin Chatterton
0140370579   £2.99

WAR BOY: A COUNTRY CHILDHOOD
Michael Foreman
0140342990   £3.50

WAR GAME *Michael Foreman*
0140371397   £3.50

THE MIDNIGHT FEAST JOKE BOOK
Shoo Rayner
0140360948   £2.99

THE YEAR I WAS BORN 1986
Sally Tagholm
0140903690   £4.99

THE YEAR I WAS BORN 1988
Sally Tagholm
0140901159   £4.99

100 QUESTIONS AND ANSWERS

CRIME AND PUNISHMENT
Anita Ganeri
0140370846   £4.50

DANGEROUS AND DEADLY
Rupert Matthews
0140374124   £3.99

**DINOSAURS AND OTHER
PREHISTORIC ANIMALS** *John Cooper*
0140364234   £3.99

EXPLORERS *Margarette Lincoln*
0140364242   £4.50

FILM & TV
Neil Cook & Kay Barnham
0140374051   £3.99

FOOTBALL
Neil Cook & Paul Harrison
0140374094   £3.99

PLANET EARTH *Roger Coote*
0140367942   £4.50

SPACE AND SPACE TRAVEL
Harry Ford & Kay Barnham
0140369503   £3.99

PONIES AND HORSES
Jenny Millington
0140376208   £4.50

RELUCTANT READERS

**TOMMY NINER AND THE PLANET
OF DANGER** *Tony Bradman*
0140346597   £3.25

FUNGUS THE BOGEYMAN
Raymond Briggs
0140542353   £5.99

**THE STINKY CHEESE MAN AND
OTHER FAIRLY STUPID TALES**
Jon Scieszka & Lane Smith
0140548963   £5.99

**STANLEY BAGSHAW AND THE TWENTY
TWO TON WHALE** *Bob Wilson*
0140504389   £3.99

GIFTED READERS

THE BEAR NOBODY WANTED
Janet & Allan Ahlberg
0140348093   £3.99

THE KINGDOM UNDER THE SEA
Joan Aiken & Jan Pieńkowski
0140306412   £4.99

THIS POEM DOESN'T RHYME
Gerard Benson (Ed)
0140342273   £3.99

UNDER THE HAWTHORN TREE
Marita Conlon-McKenna
014036031X   £3.75

10 YEARS +

At this age, children will want to make independent choices about the books they read. There are, however, ways in which you can be involved in their choices. Try reading reviews in national newspapers, get hints from other parents and keep an eye on what your children are reading. If they enjoy one Nina Bawden book, then get them another. If a particular subject appeals — for example, horror, football or ballet — try our subject index for other titles.

There is a wealth of award-winning and enduring fiction for this age group. You may recognise many of the books listed in this section from your own childhood. Quality authors write books that work on many levels. Do not discount the books that are listed in the younger age ranges. The excellent writing allows older children to gain deeper insights into the story that may have been missed at a younger age.

CHOOSING THE RIGHT BOOK

- Go for books you loved as a child that have survived today.
- Look out for favourite genres — if horror is their thing or comedy keeps them chuckling, then give them more!
- Series are always a great way to get kids reading — they try one and want the rest.
- Authors are always a key to success. We all have our favourites and so do children.
- Jackets are an important factor when choosing a book. Children will discard a book if its jacket isn't cool.
- Look out for books that have won awards, such as the Carnegie Medal, Mind Boggling Books and the Smarties Prize.
- Talk to teachers for advice, because they often spark enthusiasm for reading in the classroom.

RELUCTANT READERS

Never push reluctant readers too hard or too quickly. Many young readers are initially put off because they see reading as a competition that they never win. It is important that their reading experiences are positive and that they have fun reading. Don't worry about the number of pages read or the difficulty of the book chosen, look for quality rather than quantity with reluctant readers. They will be more interested in reading books that they have an affinity with eg. books about hobbies, favourite films or TV programmes. If the sheer visual bulk of the text in a story is off putting, try poetry which offers short, manageable verses. The rhyme, alliteration and rhythm will help them to unravel the language clues and ultimately feel more confident and successful.

GIFTED READERS

If your children are avid readers, you may have a problem keeping up with their appetite for books. It is more than likely that they will have strong opinions about what they want to read. Let them read completely through a series, they will soon discover other books which excite them equally. As well as bookshops, use your local library to extend their bookshelves. It should take them a while to work their way through the library's collection!

HINT: If the books you want are unavailable in your local bookshop, order them using the ISBN (number on barcode).

NB. All books in this section are suitable for Key Stage 2 in England and Wales National Curriculum

WATERSHIP DOWN
by Richard Adams

The classic story of a group of very human rabbits who are forced to leave their warren and undertake a long and perilous journey. This tense and gripping novel raises issues of conservation and leadership.

'Stunning, compulsive reading'
The Sunday Times

THE TROUBLE WITH DONOVAN CROFT
by Bernard Ashley

Foster brothers were all right, thought Keith, he'd had them before. But how was he to cope with Donovan, a West Indian boy who was so unhappy he wouldn't speak. A powerful story which underlines the sort of problems that any family – or any child – might have to face when the normal, secure pattern of life goes a little awry.

CARRIE'S WAR
by Nina Bawden

A story full of the right mix of plot, character and suspense. Haunted by an incident in her childhood, a grown-up 'Carrie' and her children return to the village where she and her brother Nick were evacuated during the Second World War. Only then does she discover the truth.

THE PEPPERMINT PIG
by Nina Bawden

Life seemed grim when father lost his job and the family had to move into their aunt's home. When Johnnie the pig moved in as well, things began to improve. A perceptive family story.

MOONDIAL
by Helen Cresswell

A thrilling time-slip novel in which Minty becomes inextricably caught up in a terrifying mystery. By chance she discovers the secret of the Moondial and travels back in time to perform a perilous task.

THE DEMON HEADMASTER
by Gillian Cross

On her first day at her new school Dinah realises that something is horribly wrong – all the children are strangely neat and exceptionally well behaved. With the help of her two foster brothers, Dinah is determined to unravel the secret of the sinister Headmaster.

THE GREAT ELEPHANT CHASE
by Gillian Cross

An epic novel of determination that follows Tad and Cissy's desperate race across America to save their elephant, Khush. Hiding an enormous elephant is no mean feat, but these two children show courage and perseverance as they struggle to reach their destination.

MATILDA
by Roald Dahl

Matilda is an extraordinary girl but her parents think she's a nuisance. She discovers she has an amazing power and realises that she can make trouble for the monstrous grown-ups in her life.

'Quite, quite delicious'
Mother

FIRST TERM AT TREBIZON
by Anne Digby

Fresh from a London comprehensive, Rebecca Mason is plunged into life at Trebizon, a famous boarding school for girls. The titles in this series follow the adventures of Rebecca and her friends in these modern school stories.

THE BOOK OF THE BANSHEE
by Anne Fine

Will Flowers is living in a war zone! His teenage sister, Estelle is at war with his parents. When Will's favourite author comes to school and tells them that they can write about anything, Will takes up the challenge and becomes a war reporter.

'The Book of the Banshee had me in stitches throughout'
Times Educational Supplement

GOGGLE-EYES
by Anne Fine

Anne Fine's writing is so true-to-life that readers can really identify with the young girl experiencing the break up of her family. When a new man appears around the house, Kitty can't comprehend what her mother sees in him.

SMITH
by Leon Garfield

A twelve-year-old pickpocket in 18th Century London steals a document by mistake. He finds himself caught up in a plot of murder, intrigue and betrayal that straddles the worlds of Newgate Gaol and high society.

THE OTHER FACTS OF LIFE
by Morris Gleitzman

Ben's parent's have decided that it's time to tell him the facts of life! But the facts that Ben worries about concern starving people and the environment, questions that are not easy to answer.

THE MOUSE AND HIS CHILD

by Russell Hoban

An enchanting, fast-moving tale of two wind-up mice who go on a journey to find a family. A story of courage and determination about toys and animals that is moving and accessible to children.

PAUL JENNINGS

UNDONE!

Unusual, anarchic and hilarious short stories, all with a twist. Irresistible reading, even for the most reluctant reader. Other titles from the exceptional Australian author Paul Jennings are **Unmentionable!, Unreal!, Unbelievable!, Unbearable! and Uncanny!**

THE TURBULENT TERM OF TYKE TILER

by Gene Kemp

Tyke's best friend Danny finds learning difficult, but the friends work together to enable Danny to achieve his ambition. The fun, informal language makes this story enjoyable. Each chapter begins with a joke and the book ends with a surprising twist!

A WIZARD OF EARTHSEA

by Ursula Le Guin

This classic fantasy tale of wizards, dragons, danger and courage is based on imagined islands where a nameless evil is at work. The geography is exact and so are the laws of the magic used by the wizards of the isles.

'One of the major works of fantasy in this century'
The Observer

GOODNIGHT MISTER TOM

by Michelle Magorian

Powerful and moving novel about a young city-boy evacuated during the Second World War to live with a lonely old countryman. Addressing issues of abuse and the touching relationship between the boy and his guardian, this book is unmissable.

THE HAUNTING

by Margaret Mahy

Barney is being haunted. But is he in danger? The insistent ghostly footsteps in his mind move ever closer while his sisters try to unravel the mystery. And as the supernatural events reach a tense climax, the family members learn some surprising things about themselves.

'It is the story of a powerful, frightening psychological take over. Margaret Mahy is skilled at combining magic and mystery...A gripping story'
Parents

THUNDER AND LIGHTNINGS
by Jan Mark

When Andrew's family move house, he strikes up an unexpected friendship with his neighbour, Victor. There isn't a thing Victor doesn't know about the RAF planes flying overhead. Andrew is worried when he discovers that Victor's beloved Lightnings are due to be scrapped. Beneath the simple storyline lie lasting truths about life and friendship with a message of hope for the future.

SCARY TALES TO TELL IN THE DARK
by Anthony Masters

It's a dark winter's night. Everyone should be asleep, but then someone says, 'Let's tell ghost stories.' That's just the beginning of ten haunting tales.

THE BULLY
by Jan Needle

Everyone thinks that simple, lumpy Simon Mason is a bully and a liar. He has been found guilty, sentenced and condemned without even having a proper hearing. Simon's teacher isn't convinced, but cannot understand why that nice Anna Royle would lie. She is determined to find out just who's bullying who.

TOM'S MIDNIGHT GARDEN
by Philippa Pearce

A fantasy story about Tom, who finds a secret garden in his dreams. This is very much a story about growing up, looking at things children love to which adults do not understand.

'The book is one of the finest pieces of writing for children produced since World War II...'

20th Century Children's Writers

HENRY'S LEG
by Ann Pilling

Henry wasn't looking for adventure – he had enough to contend with at home; but like it or not he finds himself at the centre of a real-life mystery, and all because of a plastic leg.

ALONG A LONELY ROAD
by Catherine Sefton

Ruth's peaceful life on the headland of Dooney is thrown into disarray when her family are taken prisoner in their own home. Ruth has to contact the outside world before it is too late.

THE SILVER SWORD
by Ian Serraillier

Based on the true story of a family of children's battle for survival in war-torn Poland. Ideal for introducing Second World War history in a way children will find dramatically compelling.

BALLET SHOES
by Noel Streatfeild

Adopted as babies Pauline, Petrova and Posy Fossil lead a sheltered life until they begin at the Children's Academy of Dancing and Stage Training. Only then do they begin to discover their special talents and extraordinary ambitions. THE book for your ballerinas or all those who enjoy a really good read.

'Her heroines are so real'
The Guardian

POETRY

THREE HAS GONE
by Jackie Kay

This collection is based on Jackie Kay's childhood memories. She writes with humour and compassion on a range of topics from favourite foods to bullying at school.

YOU TELL ME
by Roger McGough & Michael Rosen

Some of McGough and Rosen's best poetry. This is one of the funniest, most exciting books of poetry you're ever likely to read.

SILLY VERSE FOR KIDS
by Spike Milligan

The ridiculous rhymes and sensationally silly verse will amuse and amaze.

BOY AND GOING SOLO
by Roald Dahl

Dahl fans will love finding out about Roald Dahl's life which was as bizarre, frightening, exciting and funny as his stories.

ZLATA'S DIARY
by Zlata Filipovic

The real life diaries of a 10 year-old girl living in war torn Sarajevo.

'Zlata's diary...is fast becoming the book that speaks for a generation tormented by the horrors of Bosnia. It is an extraordinarily affecting volume about a girl robbed of her childhood'
The Sunday Times

FIGHTING FANTASY
by Steve Jackson & Ian Livingstone

Fighting Fantasy is an amazing reading phenomenon. These books will draw upon children's resourcefulness, decision-making and judgement skills as they playout multi-option adventure scenarios. They are not for the faint-hearted. There are intriguing problems and terrifyingly gruesome opponents as the hero dices with death and demons in search of villains, treasure and freedom.

STAYING COOL SURVIVING SCHOOL
by Rosie Rushton

The prospect of secondary school can seem daunting. Worries will be eased by this light-hearted, funny but informative look at secondary school survival strategies.

THE YEAR I WAS BORN
Compiled by Sally Tagholm

A day-by-day picture of the year your children were born. Lots of illustrations, facts, figures and information that are both amusing and useful. Children and adults will love dipping into these books.

ANNE FRANK: BEYOND THE DIARY
by Rian Verhoeven & Rudd Van Der Rol

The world behind the words. In over one hundred pictures, many never before published, Anne Frank's life before she was forced into hiding is uncovered.

THE PUFFIN FACTFILE OF KINGS AND QUEENS

by Scoular Anderson

Plenty of right royal riches in this book, from King Cnut to Elizabeth II. The sheer number of interesting facts will engage all readers.

MARMALADE ATKINS' DREADFUL DEEDS

by Andrew Davies

The ideal book for non book lovers. Marmalade Atkins is undoubtedly the worst girl in the world. If you think she's going to learn her lesson and be good by the end of the book, then you are wrong!

FANTASTIC STORIES

by Terry Jones & Michael Foreman

Satisfying short stories that are strange, thrilling, funny and even quite silly. These twenty-one original tales are illustrated in detail by Michael Foreman.

BRIAN PATTEN

GARGLING WITH JELLY

This and it's companion THAWING FROZEN FROGS are marvellously mischievous and delightfully daring collections of poems.

"A kind of poetic version of the Beano; lots of jokey energy, lots of pace and punch..."
The Times Educational Supplement

NAPPER GOES FOR GOAL

by Martin Waddell

Fun filled football stories about Napper McCann and the star players of the Red Row School Football team.

THE FUTURE-TELLING LADY
by James Berry

Each of these seven spellbinding stories has an individual voice and an irresistible energy. James Berry vividly evokes the unique history, tradition and character of the Caribbean.

AN ANGEL FOR MAY
by Melvyn Burgess

Taking refuge from his troubled life, Tam finds himself transported back in time to the Second World War. There he becomes friends with May who tries to persuade him to stay, but Tam is afraid of being permanently trapped in the past. A thrilling and moving story in which Tam gains a greater understanding of an old beggar woman through experiencing her childhood.

THE DARK IS RISING
by Susan Cooper

The powerful sense of mystery and danger is balanced against the ordinariness of daily life making this one of the best fantasy novels for children. For real fans look for the omnibus edition THE DARK IS RISING SEQUENCE

GOLD DUST
by Geraldine McCaughrean

Inez and Maro create a rumour to entice gold prospectors away from their sleepy town. A powerful but funny story about desperation, poverty and compromised ideas.

A BRIDGE TO TERABITHIA
by Katherine Paterson

It was Leslie who invented Terabithia the secret country on an island in the dark creek. Here Jess could be strong, unafraid and unbeatable. So when something terrible happens, Jess finds he can face grief and disaster better than he could ever have imagined.

CHECKLIST – BOOKS FOR CHILDREN 10 YEARS +

For your convenience we have put together the list of books featured in this section of the guide. All titles are available from bookshops. Please note prices are subject to change and some titles may become temporarily unavailable. Remember to check the author index for more books by the same author.

WATERSHIP DOWN *Richard Adams*
0140306013 £4.99

THE TROUBLE WITH DONOVAN CROFT
Bernard Ashley
0140309748 £3.99

CARRIE'S WAR *Nina Bawden*
0140306897 £3.99

THE PEPPERMINT PIG *Nina Bawden*
0140309446 £3.99

MOONDIAL *Helen Cresswell*
0140325239 £3.99

THE DEMON HEADMASTER
Gillian Cross
0140316434 £3.75

THE GREAT ELEPHANT CHASE
Gillian Cross
0140363610 £4.50

MATILDA
Roald Dahl & Quentin Blake
0140327592 £4.99

FIRST TERM AT TREBIZON
Anne Digby
0140324186 £3.50

THE BOOK OF THE BANSHEE
Anne Fine
0140347046 £3.99

GOGGLE-EYES *Anne Fine*
0140340718 £3.99

SMITH *Leon Garfield*
0140303499 £4.50

THE OTHER FACTS OF LIFE
Morris Gleitzman
0140368779 £3.50

THE MOUSE AND HIS CHILD
Russell Hoban
0140308415 £4.50

UNDONE! *Paul Jennings*
014036823X £3.50

THE TURBULENT TERM OF TYKE TILER
Gene Kemp
0140311351 £3.50

A WIZARD OF EARTHSEA
Ursula Le Guin
0140304770 £3.99

GOODNIGHT MISTER TOM
Michelle Magorian
0140315411 £4.99

THE HAUNTING *Margaret Mahy*
0140363254 £3.75

THUNDER AND LIGHTNINGS
Jan Mark
0140310630 £3.99

SCARY TALES TO TELL IN THE DARK
Anthony Masters
0140361758 £3.50

THE BULLY *Jan Needle*
0140364196 £3.99

TOM'S MIDNIGHT GARDEN
Philippa Pearce
0140308938 £3.99

HENRY'S LEG *Ann Pilling*
0140329781 £3.99

ALONG A LONELY ROAD
Catherine Sefton
0140348530 £3.50

THE SILVER SWORD *Ian Serraillier*
0140301461 £3.99

BALLET SHOES *Noel Streatfeild*
0140300414 £4.50

POETRY

THREE HAS GONE *Jackie Kay*
0140371818 £3.99

SILLY VERSE FOR KIDS
Spike Milligan
0140303316 £3.25

YOU TELL ME
Michael Rosen & Roger McGough
0140312862 £3.50

NON-FICTION

BOY AND GOING SOLO *Roald Dahl*
0140349170 £7.50

ZLATA'S DIARY *Zlata Filipovic*
0140374639 £4.50

THE FIGHTING FANTASY SERIES
Steve Jackson & Ian Livingstone

*See Puffin Catalogue for complete
list or ask your bookseller.*

THE YEAR I WAS BORN 1983
Sally Tagholm
0140902015 £4.99

THE YEAR I WAS BORN 1984
Sally Tagholm
0140902023 £4.99

STAYING COOL SURVIVING SCHOOL
Rosie Rushton
014037194X £3.99

ANNE FRANK: BEYOND THE DIARY
*Rian Verhoeven &
Rudd Van Der Rol*
0140369260 £6.99

RELUCTANT READERS

**THE PUFFIN FACTFILE OF KINGS
AND QUEENS** *Scoular Anderson*
0140363041 £3.50

**MARMALADE ATKINS'
DREADFUL DEEDS** *Andrew Davies*
0140370242 £3.25

FANTASTIC STORIES
Terry Jones & Michael Foreman
0140362762 £8.99

GARGLING WITH JELLY *Brian Patten*
0140319042 £3.50

NAPPER GOES FOR GOAL
Martin Waddell
0140313184 £3.25

GIFTED READERS

THE FUTURE-TELLING LADY
James Berry
0140347631 £3.99

AN ANGEL FOR MAY
Melvyn Burgess
0140369813 £3.75

THE DARK IS RISING
Susan Cooper
0140307990 £4.99

GOLD DUST
Geraldine McCaughrean
0140368868 £3.99

A BRIDGE TO TERABITHIA
Katherine Paterson
0140312609 £3.50

Notes

HINT: If you are unable to find a book in your local bookshop, ask them to order it using the ISBN number.

12 YEARS +

Twelve-year-olds are about to embark on the turbulent teenage years. As they try to negotiate their way into adulthood, they will be confronted with confusing issues and personal experiences. Books provide a gentle way to approach potentially difficult issues with your teenagers.

Your twelve-year-old may already be reading 'adult' books and you may feel they are not ready. There are some wonderful authors writing for teenagers today, so why not encourage them to try a few.

Teenagers and adults have similar interests. One rule when buying a book for this age group is not to patronise them. The book must look adult and not child like. Puffin's teenage reads all have contemporary cover designs and stylish black spines.

ADDRESSING ISSUES THROUGH BOOKS

The early teenage years can be filled with angst, not just for children but for parents too. Some of the books in our selection allow parents and children to step back and reassess the conflicts in their relationships with humour. Books can also act as a source of information about subjects that your children will want to discover for themselves.

There has been some controversy about 'issue' books for teenagers. Books about relationships, racism, violence, war and murder all look at the reality of life that your children will already be aware of from a multitude of different mediums. Books can offer a safe way of looking at such issues. It is not all that dissimilar from giving a toddler who is scared of having a filling a book about going to the dentist. Teenage writing guides its readers through hard-hitting issues while allowing them to empathise with characters and situations. Some of the books may contain language which is appropriate to the authors' subject matter.

Try to keep an eye on what your children are reading as you may feel that some of the issues addressed are too hard hitting and grown up for them to cope with. We have marked books in this section that you may want to read before passing on to your teenager with a *. However, these books are widely available in schools and libraries and are written with this age group in mind.

CHOOSING THE RIGHT BOOK

- Books that have good contemporary covers and that you know will appeal to your children.
- Books about issues that your children may be worried about.
- Books that are fun, as well as serious.
- Let your children read what they want. You can suggest and buy books as presents, but ultimately the choice is theirs.

RELUCTANT READERS

The teenage reluctant reader requires material simple enough to be accessible, but relevant enough to interest them. Look for amusing books about the teenage experience that they will be able to relate to. The computer revolution has generated a new form of literature that most teenagers are familiar with. They may be more at ease with books that exploit this link. Choose-your-own adventure books like the Fighting Fantasy series present a reluctant reader with a new way of reading that may spark interest. Graphic or comic strip novels are other forms of literature that are accessible to teenagers. They are ideal for reluctant readers as they present many visual clues, a short narrative or dialogue with a more complex text or meaning.

GIFTED READERS

Gifted readers will challenge established ideas and toy with potentially difficult issues within the safe context of fiction. That is why the science fiction and fantasy genres are often immensely popular with gifted readers.

Many classics were originally written for adults, but are excellent for stimulating gifted readers. They will delight in the historical details as well as immersing themselves in the unfamiliar language.

HINT: Adverts for other titles by the same author or for the same readership can be found in many Puffin Books.

12 YEARS + BOOKS FOR TEENAGE READERS

ONE MORE RIVER
by Lynne Reid Banks

Life in Canada had always been safe and happy for Lesley Shelby. Then one day her father announced that they were moving to Israel to live on a kibbutz. As well as being a perceptive story about a girl growing up, it is a lucid and living picture of the agonies and confusions which accompany divided loyalties.

THE REAL PLATO JONES
by Nina Bawden

Plato Jones is confused, is he Greek like his mother or Welsh like his father? Plato wants to discover the truth about his family's past and begins to uncover the wartime activities of his grandfathers in the process. This is a story about a young boy growing up and discovering who he really is.

'A cracking good read. It's dramatic and tense, with a blistering climax that'll have you turning the pages like a mini tornado. Highly recommended.'
Daily Telegraph

THE GUARDIANS
by John Christopher

A chilling story of life in the not-too-distant future, when power is held by a few and rebellion is crushed mercilessly. On the run after the tragic death of his father, Rob Randall is afraid of being captured and punished. In desperation he crosses the Barrier into the open fields of the County, where life appears idyllic.

NOT DRESSED LIKE THAT, YOU DON'T!
by Yvonne Coppard

An hilarious diary account of life for a teenage girl and her long-suffering mother. A book that will strike a chord in many households.

'A wickedly funny book... This book is a must – easy to get into, impossible to stop reading'
The Independent on Sunday

DON'T LOOK BEHIND YOU
by Lois Duncan

Suddenly everything is different in April Corrigan's life. Her boyfriend, her friends, her tennis, even her long blonde hair – gone. Everything evaporates when her father is shot at and her family are forced to go into hiding. A highly charged story by a master of suspense.

ANNE FINE

FLOUR BABIES

Simon Martin and his class face up to parental responsibility when they have to look after sacks of flour as part of a science project.

'I have read and re-read Flour Babies, Anne Fine's wise and exuberant comedy...and it gets better each time'
The Times

MADAME DOUBTFIRE

'I hope children that see the film will want to read the book too. Films can only show what happens, but a book can tell you how and why, and the way everyone feels'
Anne Fine

THE FRIENDS
by Rosa Guy

Phyllisia Cathy arrives in Harlem from the West Indies and finds inner-city life and school difficult to say the least. Only Edith Jackson is friendly to her, but her scruffy appearance puts Phyllisia off. Eventually the girls become close and supportive friends.

BUDDY
by Nigel Hinton

A sensitive look at the breakup of a family and its effect on an adolescent boy.

'It is compassionately written, genuinely moving and can be highly recommended'
School Librarian

BASKETBALL GAME
by Julius Lester

Allen is black and Rebecca is white, and in Nashville, Tennessee, in 1956 that means they must be kept apart. They like each other but can their relationship survive the deeply rooted prejudice that surrounds them?

JOAN LINGARD

THE TWELFTH DAY OF JULY

Kevin and Sadie know their relationship is dangerous. This is the first of Joan Lingard's stories about the young Belfast couple. The books can be read on their own or as part of a series.

MARGARET MAHY

MEMORY

Tackling the alarming subject of dementia and death with understanding and gentle humour. *Memory* is a book whose depth and social awareness make it a story for all.

The queen of children's fiction'
The Independent on Sunday

A PACK OF LIES
by Geraldine McCaughrean

Twelve stories in one, all told by MCC Berkshire, the mysterious stranger who moves into Ailsa and her mother's antique shop. He is rather out of the ordinary and irresistibly charming, so much so that he manages to keep customers spellbound with his extravagant stories and sells them antiques into the bargain.

'Sparkling with wit and originality'
The Guardian

A MIDSUMMER NIGHT'S DEATH
by K M Peyton

Mr Robinson's Death looks like suicide...but is it really murder? Jonathan becomes suspicious about the circumstances of his English Master's death, when he realises that one of the other masters, Charles Hugo, has lied to the police. An absorbing thriller.

RUBY IN THE SMOKE *
by Philip Pullman

When Sally Lockhart becomes an orphan, she is in greater danger than she can possibly know. These fast-paced and authentically detailed thrillers are set in the busy thoroughfares and dank, smoggy backstreets of Victorian London.

BROTHER IN THE LAND
by Robert Swindells

Danny and his brother have come through a nuclear holocaust alive, only to discover that the world has gone sour in more ways than one. This is a hard-hitting story of survival against the odds that makes the whole issue seem alarmingly urgent.

STONE COLD *
by Robert Swindells

This is a tense, exciting thriller. Swindells creates a perceptive and harrowing portrait of life on the streets, as a serial killer preys on the young and vulnerable homeless.

MILDRED D TAYLOR

ROLL OF THUNDER, HEAR MY CRY

Mississippi in the 1930s is a hard place for a girl – especially when she is black. The first of three stories based on the author's own family history. Through nine-year-old Cassie's eyes, the reader sees how racism permeates lives.

FIREWEED
by Jill Paton Walsh

Bill and Julie would never have met if it hadn't been wartime. An unforgettable and poignant story of two teenagers adrift in London during the Blitz.

THE SCARECROWS *
by Robert Westall

While reluctantly spending the summer at his hated stepfather's house, Simon Wood takes refuge from family pressures in the old mill house across the field. Simon knows that although the mill has been empty since 1943 there is someone or something watching and waiting, but for what? When the scarecrows appear, he knows that the time has come to face a terrifying test.

URN BURIAL *
by Robert Westall

When Ralph discovers a weird 'tomb' he investigates further. Before he knows it he has awakened a dangerous and terrifying secret that threatens to wreak havoc in the community.

POETRY

IN TIME OF WAR
Edited by Anne Harvey

A world of bombs, blackouts and broken relationships, of patriotism, propaganda and unforgotten pain. These poems from both the First and Second World Wars take you right to the heart of the world at war.

'This is a marvellous collection of poets'
The Guardian

STRICTLY PRIVATE
Edited by Roger McGough

Keep out of this book if you like dissecting dusty old verse, for this is a collection of today's poetry that is fresh and very much alive! Roger McGough has gathered together a richly varied anthology of contemporary poems.

'Any youngster will find something that speaks directly to him'
The Guardian

TALKING TURKEYS
by Benjamin Zephaniah

Hot, hip playful and provocative, here are straight-talking poems from a ground-breaking rap poet. Look forward to a powerful performance on every page.

NON-FICTION

CATHERINE
by Maureen Dunbar

Anorexia nervosa is more than an illness, its consequences affect the whole family. Here Catherine's mother recounts through her diaries her daughter's seven-year fight against this devastating disease. A true story about an intelligent, sensitive girl's struggle for life.

THIRTEEN SOMETHING
by Jane Goldman

Life's not easy when you're thirteen something... Help is at hand in this brilliant collection of advice, facts and hints.

RELUCTANT READERS

I FELL IN LOVE WITH A LEATHER JACKET
by Steve Barlow & Steve Skidmore

Sammy, a confused conservationist, confesses her innermost secrets to her best friend Camille, through a series of letters. A witty and encouraging book for all those wrestling with teenage idealism.

MAUS 1: A SURVIVOR'S TALE MAUS 11:
by Art Speigleman

Two sophisticated books for reluctant readers who respond to the graphic novel format. Maus is the story of a Jewish survivor of Hitler's Europe; his son, a cartoonist, tries to come to terms with his father and his terrifying story.

WHO SAYS ANIMALS DON'T HAVE RIGHTS?
by Jean Ure

Penny is being held to ransom. Her kidnappers don't want money they just want to force her uncle to reveal the truth about his company's animal experiments. A hard hitting drama that raises many questions for the reader and shows that there is rarely an easy answer.

GIFTED READERS

THE DAY THEY CAME TO ARREST THE BOOK
by Nat Hentoff

When an attempt is made to ban Huckleberry Finn from an American school because of alleged racism, the ensuing row rapidly involves the whole community. A powerful novel about the dangers of looking at classic literature through the blinkers of political correctness and special interests.

THE WAVE
by Morton Rhue

A Nazi style system sweeps through an American high school when a classroom history experiment goes too far. This chilling novel is based on a true story.

I WAS THERE
by Hans Peter Richter

'I am reporting how I lived through that time and what I saw – no more. I was there. I Believed – and I will never believe again' Hans Peter Richter

A startling insight into the attitudes of young people and their responses to the events of the Third Reich.

CHECKLIST - BOOKS FOR TEENAGE READERS 12 YEARS +

For your convenience we have put together the list of books featured in this section of the guide. All titles are available from bookshops. Please note prices are subject to change and some titles may become temporarily unavailable. Remember to check the author index for more books by the same author.

ONE MORE RIVER *Lynne Reid Banks*
0140370218   £4.99

THE REAL PLATO JONES
Nina Bawden
0140368477   £3.99

THE GUARDIANS *John Christopher*
0140305793   £4.99

NOT DRESSED LIKE THAT, YOU DON'T!
Yvonne Coppard
0140371788   £3.50

DON'T LOOK BEHIND YOU
Lois Duncan
0140372938   £4.50

FLOUR BABIES *Anne Fine*
0140361472   £3.99

MADAME DOUBTFIRE *Anne Fine*
0140373551   £4.50

THE FRIENDS *Rosa Guy*
014037177X   £4.99

BUDDY *Nigel Hinton*
0140371761   £4.25

BASKETBALL GAME *Julius Lester*
0140373322   £3.50

THE TWELFTH DAY OF JULY
Joan Lingard
0140371753   £3.99

MEMORY
Margaret Mahy
0140373047   £4.99

A PACK OF LIES
Geraldine McCaughrean
0140373055   £4.50

A MIDSUMMER NIGHT'S DEATH
K M Peyton
0140372148   £4.50

THE RUBY IN THE SMOKE
Philip Pullman
014036627X   £3.99

BROTHER IN THE LAND
Robert Swindells
0140373004   £4.50

STONE COLD *Robert Swindells*
0140362517   £3.99

ROLL OF THUNDER, HEAR MY CRY
Mildred D Taylor
0140371745   £4.99

FIREWEED *Jill Paton Walsh*
0140305602   £3.50

THE SCARECROWS *Robert Westall*
014037308X   £4.50

URN BURIAL *Robert Westall*
0140373179   £4.99

POETRY

IN TIME OF WAR *Anne Harvey (Ed)*
0140373721   £4.99

STRICTLY PRIVATE
Roger McGough (Ed)
0140328319   £4.99

TALKING TURKEYS
Benjamin Zephaniah
0140363300   £3.50

NON-FICTION

CATHERINE *Maureen Dunbar*
0140342230   £5.99

THIRTEEN SOMETHING *Jane Goldman*
0140371958   £4.25

RELUCTANT READERS

**I FELL IN LOVE WITH A
LEATHER JACKET**
Steve Barlow & Steve Skidmore
0140366350   £3.50

MAUS 1: A SURVIVOR'S TALE
Art Speigleman
0140173153   £9.99

MAUS 11 *Art Spiegleman*
0140132066   £9.99

**WHO SAYS ANIMALS DON'T
HAVE RIGHTS?** *Jean Ure*
0140366563   £3.50

GIFTED READERS

**THE DAY THEY CAME TO
ARREST THE BOOK**
Nat Hentoff
0140373144   £4.50

THE WAVE *Morton Rhue*
0140371885   £3.75

I WAS THERE *Hans Peter Richter*
014032206X   £3.99

Notes

HINT: If you are unable to find a book in your local bookshop, ask them to order it using the ISBN number.

PUFFIN MODERN CLASSICS

"Do not deprive your child by withholding any of them." **The Sunday Times**

- Puffin Modern Classics provide a library stocked with the very best in children's contemporary fiction.
- Puffin Modern Classics have strong writing, vivid characters and gripping storylines..
- They are written by a range of bestselling and award-winning authors.
- The contemporary covers make them highly collectable and great presents.
- The series is suitable for readers 8 years +.
- Young Puffin Modern Classics are available for children aged 6 years +.

These are the classics of the future.

HINT: Look out for the **MC** sign in the age-ranged sections.

PUFFIN CLASSICS
The Essential Collection

"Don't be put off by the fact that they've been around for ages, it's because they're so good that they've stood the test of time." **The Daily Telegraph**

- Puffin publishes the widest range of complete and unabridged classics for children available today with over 90 titles available.

- The Puffin Classics series contains fiction and poetry that has earned the title "classic" through the quality of the writing, compelling storylines and strong characterisation.

- Every Puffin Classic comes with an introduction which provides a biographical note on the author and the historical context in which the book was written. Perfect for all those struggling with school projects.

- All titles in the series fulfill the National Curriculum requirements for children to read some long-established children's fiction.

- With distinctive and stylish covers. Puffin Classics are extremely collectable and the text is designed for accessibility and readability.

Books from the past for children of the present.

PUFFIN MODERN CLASSICS

YOUNG PUFFIN MODERN CLASSICS

6+ YEARS

MRS PEPPERPOT IN THE MAGIC WOOD
Alf Prøysen

CLEVER POLLY AND THE STUPID WOLF
Catherine Storr

ADVENTURES OF THE LITTLE WOODEN HORSE
Ursula Moray Williams

PUFFIN MODERN CLASSICS

8+ YEARS

A NECKLACE OF RAINDROPS
Joan Aiken/Jan Pieńkowski

THE CHILDREN OF GREEN KNOWE
Lucy M Boston

THE MIDNIGHT FOX
by Betsy Byars

STIG OF THE DUMP
Clive King

THE FOX BUSTERS
Dick King-Smith

THUNDER AND LIGHTNINGS
Jan Mark

THE BORROWERS
Mary Norton

MRS FRISBY AND THE RATS OF NIMH
Robert C O'Brien

A DOG SO SMALL
Philippa Pearce

CHARLOTTE'S WEB
E B White

TARKA THE OTTER
Henry Williamson

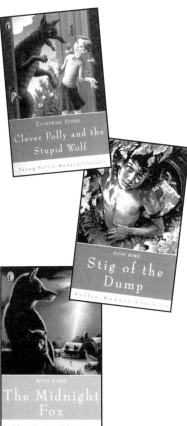

PUFFIN CLASSICS

LITTLE WOMEN
Louisa M Alcott

PETER PAN
J M Barrie

JANE EYRE
Charlotte Brontë

WUTHERING HEIGHTS
Emily Brontë

LITTLE LORD FAUNTLEROY
Frances Hodgson Burnett

THE SECRET GARDEN
Frances Hodgson Burnett

**ALICE'S ADVENTURES
IN WONDERLAND**
Lewis Carroll

THROUGH THE LOOKING GLASS
Lewis Carroll

A CHRISTMAS CAROL
Charles Dickens

OLIVER TWIST (ABRIDGED)
Charles Dickens

**THE HOUND OF
THE BASKERVILLES**
Sir Arthur Conan Doyle

MOONFLEET
J Meade Falkner

THE WIND IN THE WILLOWS
Kenneth Grahame

KING ARTHUR AND HIS KNIGHTS OF THE ROUND TABLE
Roger Lancelyn Green

TALES OF THE GREEK HEROES
Roger Lancelyn Green

THE JUNGLE BOOK
Rudyard Kipling

JUST SO STORIES
Rudyard Kipling

TALES FROM SHAKESPEARE
Charles and Mary Lamb

THE PHANTOM OF THE OPERA
Gaston Leroux

THE CALL OF THE WILD
Jack London

WHITE FANG
Jack London

ANNE OF GREEN GABLES
LM Montgomery

THE RAILWAY CHILDREN
E Nesbit

POLLYANNA
Eleanor H Porter

BLACK BEAUTY
Anna Sewell

FRANKENSTEIN
Mary Shelley

TREASURE ISLAND
Robert Louis Stevenson

THE ADVENTURES OF TOM SAWYER
Mark Twain

JOURNEY TO THE CENTRE OF THE EARTH
Jules Verne

THE HAPPY PRINCE AND OTHER STORIES
Oscar Wilde

SEE BACK OF GUIDE FOR MONEY-OFF VOUCHER

CHECKLIST – PUFFIN MODERN CLASSICS

For your convenience we have put together the list of books featured in this section of the guide. All titles are available from bookshops. Please note prices are subject to change and some titles may become temporarily unavailable. Remember to check the author index for more books by the same author.

6+ YEARS

MRS PEPPERPOT IN THE MAGIC WOOD
Alf Prøysen
0140372482 £3.99

CLEVER POLLY AND THE STUPID WOLF
Catherine Storr
0140364633 £3.50

ADVENTURES OF THE LITTLE WOODEN HORSE
Ursula Moray Williams
0140366091 £4.50

8+ YEARS

A NECKLACE OF RAINDROPS
Joan Aiken & Jan Pieńkowski
014036613X £3.99

THE CHILDREN OF GREEN KNOWE
Lucy M Boston
0140364617 £4.50

THE MIDNIGHT FOX *Betsy Byars*
0140370331 £4.50

STIG OF THE DUMP *Clive King*
0140364501 £4.99

THE FOX BUSTERS *Dick King-Smith*
0140372326 £3.99

THUNDER AND LIGHTNINGS
Jan Mark
0140366172 £4.25

THE BORROWERS *Mary Norton*
014036451X £4.99

MRS FRISBY AND THE RATS OF NIMH
Robert O'Brien
0140366148 £4.99

A DOG SO SMALL *Philippa Pearce*
0140372342 £4.99

CHARLOTTE'S WEB *E B White*
0140364498 £4.99

TARKA THE OTTER *Henry Williamson*
0140366210 £4.99

10+ YEARS

WATERSHIP DOWN *Richard Adams*
0140364536 £5.99

CARRIE'S WAR *Nina Bawden*
0140364560 £4.99

THE DARK IS RISING *Susan Cooper*
0140364625 £4.99

GRINNY *Nicholas Fisk*
0140372350 £3.99

SMITH *Leon Garfield*
0140364587 £4.50

THE MOUSE AND HIS CHILD
Russell Hoban
0140364552 £4.50

THE TURBULENT TERM OF TYKE TILER
Gene Kemp
0140366105 £4.50

A WIZARD OF EARTHSEA
Ursula Le Guin
0140364609 £4.99

A WRINKLE IN TIME
Madeleine L'Engle
0140372318 £4.99

GOODNIGHT MR TOM
Michelle Magorian
0140372334 £5.99

A BRIDGE TO TERABITHIA
Katherine Paterson
0140366180 £4.99

TOM'S MIDNIGHT GARDEN
Philippa Pearce
0140364544 £4.99

FLAMBARDS *K M Peyton*
0140366229 £5.99

THE SILVER SWORD *Ian Serraillier*
0140364528 £4.99

BALLET SHOES *Noel Streatfeild*
0140364595 £4.99

THE EAGLE OF THE NINTH
Rosemary Sutcliff
0140364579 £4.99

THE CAY *Theodore Taylor*
0140366202 £3.99

THE DOLPHIN CROSSSING
Jill Paton Walsh
0140366245 £4.50

12+ YEARS (TEENAGE)

THE FRIENDS *Rosa Guy*
0140366164 £4.99

ROLL OF THUNDER, HEAR MY CRY
Mildred D Taylor
0140366253 £5.50

CHECKLIST – PUFFIN CLASSICS

For your convenience we have put together the list of books featured in this section of the guide. All titles are available from bookshops. Please note prices are subject to change and some titles may become temporarily unavailable. Remember to check the author index for more books by the same author.

CLASSICS

LITTLE WOMEN *Louisa M Alcott*
0140366687 £2.99

PETER PAN *J M Barrie*
0140366741 £2.99

JANE EYRE *Charlotte Brontë*
0140366784 £2.99

WUTHERING HEIGHTS *Emily Brontë*
0140366946 £2.99

LITTLE LORD FAUNTLEROY
Frances Hodgson Burnett
0140367535 £2.99

THE SECRET GARDEN
Frances Hodgson Burnett
0140366660 £2.50

ALICE'S ADVENTURES IN WONDERLAND
Lewis Carroll
014036675X £2.99

THROUGH THE LOOKING GLASS
Lewis Carroll
0140367098 £2.99

A CHRISTMAS CAROL *Charles Dickens*
0140367233 £2.50

OLIVER TWIST (*abridged*)
Charles Dickens
0140368140 £2.99

THE HOUND OF THE BASKERVILLES
Sir Arthur Conan Doyle
0140366997 £2.99

MOONFLEET *J Meade Falkner*
0140367047 £3.50

THE WIND IN THE WILLOWS
Kenneth Grahame
0140366857 £2.99

KING ARTHUR AND HIS KNIGHTS OF THE ROUND TABLE
Roger Lancelyn Green
0140366709 £4.50

TALES OF THE GREEK HEROES
Roger Lancelyn Green
0140366830 £3.99

THE JUNGLE BOOK *Rudyard Kipling*
0140366865 £2.99

JUST SO STORIES *Rudyard Kipling*
0140367020 £2.99

TALES FROM SHAKESPEARE
Charles and Mary Lamb
0140366776 £4.99

THE PHANTOM OF THE OPERA
Gaston Leroux
0140368132 £3.50

THE CALL OF THE WILD *Jack London*
0140366695 £2.50

WHITE FANG *Jack London*
0140366679 £2.99

ANNE OF GREEN GABLES
LM Montgomery
0140367411 £3.50

THE RAILWAY CHILDREN *E Nesbit*
0140366717 £2.50

POLLYANNA *Eleanor H Porter*
0140366822 £2.99

BLACK BEAUTY *Anna Sewell*
0140366849 £2.99

FRANKENSTEIN *Mary Shelley*
0140367128 £3.50

TREASURE ISLAND
Robert Louis Stevenson
0140366725 £2.99

THE ADVENTURES OF TOM SAWYER
Mark Twain
0140366733 £2.99

JOURNEY TO THE CENTRE OF THE EARTH
Jules Verne
0140367152 £3.50

THE HAPPY PRINCE AND OTHER STORIES
Oscar Wilde
0140366911 £2.99

SEE BACK OF PARENT'S GUIDE FOR PUFFIN CLASSICS AND PUFFIN MODERN CLASSICS MONEY-OFF VOUCHER

FURTHER
READING

National Curriculum

Books for Parents

NATIONAL CURRICULUM FOR ENGLAND AND WALES

English is one of the three core subjects in the National Curriculum that lays down the fundamental skills children should develop as they progress through their school career.

Speaking and listening, writing and reading are the three components of the English Curriculum. Reading is an area where you as a parent can help significantly. In fact, recent government reports have stated:

'PARENTAL SUPPORT FOR READING IS VITAL'

As a parent it is essential to know what books your children should be reading. The National Curriculum states that children should read a whole range of literature, including poems, stories, folk tales, myths, legends and picture books.

KEY STAGE 1
AGE 5–7 YEARS

At Key Stage 1 the National Curriculum states that your child's reading should cover the following:

- poems and stories with familiar settings and those based on imaginary or fantasy worlds;

- books and poems written by significant children's authors;

- retellings of traditional stories, folk and fairy stories;

- stories from a range of cultures;

- stories, poems and chants containing patterned and predictable language;

- and finally stories and poems which are particularly challenging in terms of length and vocabulary.

KEY STAGE 2
AGE 8–11 YEARS

Whilst progressing through Key Stage 2 your children should read a good selection of the following:

- a range of modern fiction by significant children's authors;

- some long-established children's fiction;

- a range of modern poetry;

- some classic poetry;

- books drawn from a variety of cultures and traditions;

- myths, legends and traditional stories.

KEY STAGES 3 & 4
AGE 12–16 YEARS

- plays by Shakespeare and other major dramatists;

- works of fiction by major writers published before 1900;

- works of fiction by well-established writers published after 1900;

- a range of poetry by major poets published before 1900;

- poems by major poets published after 1900;

- and finally a range of non-literary and non-fiction texts.

A full list of titles suitable for the National Curriculum is available from Puffin Books.

BABIES NEED BOOKS
by Dorothy Butler

The book for all parents concerned about reading. Filled with practical advice about how to encourage your children to develop a love of reading.

LISTEN TO YOUR CHILD
by David Crystal

Learning to talk is a milestone in a child's development and a deeply moving and often hilarious, experience for all parents. David Crystal's guide to children's language will help parents to understand the complete process of language development.

CREATIVE PLAY
by Dorothy Einon

Psychologist Dorothy Einon has written a book for parents and teachers that offers hundreds of ideas for play and games.

'A delightful and thoroughly practical book to help any parent discover how to stimulate a small child's senses and ability to learn from birth onwards'
Sheila Kitzinger

PENELOPE LEACH

BABYHOOD : INFANT DEVELOPMENT

'A superbly comprehensive guide to child development in a form accessible to any interested reader, I can't recommend Babyhood *too highly'*
World Medicine

BABY AND CHILD

The comprehensive, authoritative and practical handbook on the first five years of life.

THE PARENTS' A TO Z

Whether your children are boys or girls, six months, six years or sixteen years, they will present you with an endless series of decisions, from whether to call the doctor to what approach to take to discipline.

THE READING SOLUTION
by Paul Kropp with Wendy Cooling

It is vital that children become and remain readers. This key book, complete with booklists, helps parents stimulate a love of reading for life.

SUBJECT
INDEX

SUBJECT INDEX

BULLYING

BUSES, TRAINS & CARS

CATS & DOGS

COMIC STRIP

COMPUTERS & COMPUTER GAMES

CONSERVATION & ENVIRONMENT

COUNTING & NUMBERS

NOAH AND THE RABBITS *Sally Kilroy* 2,7
THIS LITTLE PUFFIN... *Elizabeth Matterson* 5,8
TEN LITTLE TEDDY BEARS *Maureen Roffey* 6,8

DEATH

WATERSHIP DOWN *Richard Adams* 39,47,58,61
CARRIE'S WAR *Nina Bawden* 39,47,58,61
SNOWMAN, THE *Raymond Briggs* 3,7
SECRET GARDEN, THE *Frances Hodgson Burnett* 59,62
GUARDIANS, THE *John Christopher* 49,55
MOONDIAL *Helen Cresswell* 39,47
GREAT ELEPHANT CHASE, THE *Gillian Cross* 40,47
BOY AND GOING SOLO *Roald Dahl* 44,48
WITCHES, THE *Roald Dahl* 30,37
OLIVER TWIST *Charles Dickens* 59,62
CATHERINE *Maureen Dunbar* 53,55
GOODNIGHT MR TOM *Michelle Magorian* 41,47,58,61
MEMORY *Margaret Mahy* 51,55
BRIDGE TO TERABITHIA *Katherine Paterson* 46,48,58,61
MIDSUMMER NIGHT'S DEATH, A *K M Peyton* 51,55
POLLYANNA *Eleanor H Porter* 60,62
RUBY IN THE SMOKE, THE *Philip Pullman* 51,55
ROSA'S SINGING GRANDFATHER *Leon Rosselson* 26,27
FRED *Posy Simmonds* 12,15,26,28
BROTHER IN THE LAND *Robert Swindells* 51,55
STONE COLD *Robert Swindells* 51,55
GOING WEST 12,15
Martin Waddell & Philippe Dupasquier
CHARLOTTE'S WEB *E B White* 32,37,57,61

DINOSAURS

DINOSAURS AND OTHER PREHISTORIC ANIMALS 35,38
John Cooper
DINOSAURS AND ALL THAT RUBBISH 10,15
Michael Foreman
LONG NECK AND THUNDER FOOT 11,15
Helen Piers & Michael Foreman
DINOSAUR ROAR! *Paul & Henrietta Stickland* 5,8
JOURNEY TO THE CENTRE OF THE EARTH 60,62
Jules Verne

DIVORCE, SEPARATION & SINGLE PARENTS

REAL PLATO JONES, THE *Nina Bawden* 49,55
FLOUR BABIES *Anne Fine* 50,55
GOGGLE-EYES *Anne Fine* 40,47
MADAME DOUBTFIRE *Anne Fine* 50,55
GOING TO PLAYSCHOOL (Series) *Sarah Garland* 4,7
BUDDY *Nigel Hinton* 50,55
TWIG THING, THE *Jan Mark* 21,27
RAILWAY CHILDREN, THE *E Nesbit* 60,62
HENRY'S LEG *Ann Pilling* 42,47
KASPER IN THE GLITTER *Philip Ridley* 32,37
METEORITE SPOON *Philip Ridley* 32,37
STONE COLD *Robert Swindells* 51,55

FAIRY TALES & NURSERY RHYMES
(including unusual tellings)

EACH PEACH PEAR PLUM *Janet & Allan Ahlberg* 3,7
REVOLTING RHYMES *Roald Dahl* 17,27
FAIRY TALES *Terry Jones & Michael Foreman* 26,28
THE BEAST WITH A THOUSAND TEETH 10,15
Terry Jones & Michael Foreman
THIS LITTLE PUFFIN... *Elizabeth Matterson (Ed)* 5,8
NICE WORK, LITTLE WOLF! *Hilda Offen* 11,15
LITTLE RED RIDING HOOD *Tony Ross* 13,16
STINKY CHEESEMAN AND OTHER FAIRLY STUPID 36,38
TALES, THE *Jon Scieszka & Lane Smith*
TRUE STORY OF THE 3 LITTLE PIGS, THE 17,27
Jon Scieszka & Lane Smith
CLEVER POLLY AND THE STUPID WOLF 23,28,57,61
Catherine Storr
HAPPY PRINCE & OTHER STORIES, THE *Oscar Wilde* 60,62
SELFISH GIANT, THE 12,15
Oscar Wilde, Michael Foreman & Freire Wright
DO-IT-YOURSELF HOUSE THAT JACK 12,15,26,28
BUILT, THE *John Yeoman & Quentin Blake*

FAMILIES

WATERSHIP DOWN *Richard Adams* 39,47,58,61
HAPPY FAMILIES SERIES *Allan Ahlberg* 18,27
BABY'S CATALOGUE, THE *Janet & Allan Ahlberg* 1,7
PEEPO *Janet & Allan Ahlberg* 1,7
TROUBLE WITH DONOVAN CROFT, THE *Bernard Ashley* 39,47
ONE MORE RIVER *Lynne Reid Banks* 49,55
CARRIE'S WAR *Nina Bawden* 39,47,58,61
PEPPERMINT PIG, THE *Nina Bawden* 39,47
REAL PLATO JONES, THE *Nina Bawden* 49,55
MIDNIGHT FOX, THE *Betsy Byars* 29,37,57,61
WINNI ALLFOURS *Babette Cole* 9,15
DARK IS RISING, THE *Susan Cooper* 46,48,58,61
A GIFT FROM WINKLESEA *Helen Cresswell* 20,27
DEMON HEADMASTER, THE *Gillian Cross* 39,47
UNDER THE HAWTHORN TREE 36,38
Marita Conlon-McKenna
GREAT ELEPHANT CHASE, THE *Gillian Cross* 40,47
MATILDA *Roald Dahl* 40,47
CATHERINE *Maureen Dunbar* 53,55
DON'T LOOK BEHIND YOU *Lois Duncan* 49,55
BOOK OF THE BANSHEE, THE *Anne Fine* 40,47
FLOUR BABIES *Anne Fine* 50,55
GOGGLE-EYES *Anne Fine* 40,47
MADAME DOUBTFIRE *Anne Fine* 50,55
PATCHWORK QUILT, THE 13,16
Valerie Flournoy & Jerry Pinkney
GOING TO PLAYSCHOOL *Sarah Garland* 4,7
OTHER FACTS OF LIFE, THE *Morris Gleitzman* 40,47
BUDDY *Nigel Hinton* 50,55
MOUSE AND HIS CHILD, THE *Russell Hoban* 41,47,58,61
LUCY & TOMS a.b.c. *Shirley Hughes* 4,7
TITCH *Pat Hutchins* 4,7
GRANNY'S QUILT *Penny Ives* 10,15

8

FANTASY

FATHERS

FEAR & WORRY

FOOD, DRINK & EATING

FRIENDSHIP

GENDER (NON-STEREOTYPICAL STORIES)

GHOSTS

GIFTED READERS

2

INSECTS (See BIRDS AND INSECTS)

JEALOUSY

LONELINESS

LOVE

MOTHERS

TV & FILM

WITCHES, WIZARDS & MAGIC

WAR & CONFLICT

AUTHOR
INDEX

AUTHOR INDEX

The author index includes all of the titles featured in the Guide, listed by age range. These titles are followed by a list of other books by this author that are suitable for the age group of the featured title. Look at the relevant page for the age range.

With thanks to the following illustrators

The page numbers quoted relate to the page in the Parent's Guide where the illustrations appear.

© **AFF/ANNE FRANK STICHTING, AMSTERDAM** 1992 Anne Frank: Beyond the Diary *by Rian Verhoeven and Rudd Van Der Rol p.44*

© **JANET AHLBERG** 1982 The Baby's Catalogue *by Janet and Allan Ahlberg p.1*

© **JANET AHLBERG** 1978 Each Peach Pear Plum *by Janet and Allan Ahlberg p.3*

© **JANET AHLBERG** 1981 Peepo! *by Janet and Allan Ahlberg p.1*

© **JANET AHLBERG** 1988 Starting School *by Janet and Allan Ahlberg p.9*

© **JANET AHLBERG** 1988 Mrs Wobble and the Waitress *by Janet and Allan Ahlberg p.18*

© **JANET AHLBERG** 1992 The Bear Nobody Wanted *by Janet and Allan Ahlberg p.36*

© **PAMELA ALLEN** 1982 Who Sank the Boat? *by Pamela Allen p.3*

© **SCOULAR ANDERSON** 1993 The Puffin Factfile of Kings and Queens *by Scoular Anderson p.45*

© **ROS ASQUITH** 1991 Not Dressed Like That You Don't *by Yvonne Coppard p.49*

© **SIAN BAILEY** 1993 The Borrowers *by Mary Norton p.58*

© **ROWAN BARNES-MURPHY** 1988 Adventure on Skull Island *by Tony Bradman p.22*

© **JEAN BAYLIS** 1988 Dustbin Charlie *by Ann Pilling p.21*

© **JEAN BAYLIS** 1989 Stranger Danger *by Anne Fine* p.20

© **LINDA BIRCH** 1987 The Hodgeheg *by Dick King-Smith p.22*

© **QUENTIN BLAKE** 1993 (cover) Boy and Going Solo *by Roald Dahl p.44*

© **QUENTIN BLAKE** 1994 The Do-It-Yourself House that Jack Built *by John Yeoman & Quentin Blake p.12*

© **QUENTIN BLAKE** 1993 Featherbrains *by John Yeoman and Quentin Blake p.23*

© **QUENTIN BLAKE** 1988 Matilda *by Roald Dahl p.40*

© **QUENTIN BLAKE** Quick, Let's Get Out of Here! *by Michael Rosen p.33*

© **QUENTIN BLAKE** 1983 The Witches *by Roald Dahl p.30*

© **EMILIE BOON** 1988 Mummy, Where Are You? *by Harriet Ziefert p.2*

© **MAUREEN BRADLEY** 1992 The Go-Ahead Gang *by Robert Swindells p.23*

© **RAYMOND BRIGGS** 1969 The Elephant and the Bad Baby *by Elfrida Vipont p.5*

© **RUUD BRUIJN** 1987 Henry's Leg *by Ann Pilling p.42*

© **ROD CAMPBELL** 1982 Dear Zoo *by Rod Campbell p.1*

© **JONATHAN CAPE** 1968 A Necklace of Raindrops *by Joan Aiken & Jan Pienkowski p.29*

© **ERIC CARLE** 1977 The Bad-Tempered Ladybird *by Eric Carle p.9*

© **MARTIN CHATTERTON** 1994 The Nutty Footy Book *by Martin Chatterton p.34*

© **BABETTE COLE** 1993 Winni Allfours *by Babette Cole p.9*

© **PENNY DANN** 1991 No Hickory No Dickory No Dock *by John Agard and Grace Nichols p.26*

© **JO DAVIES** 1986 Dumpling *by Dick King-Smith & Jo Davies p.19*

© **GRAHAM DEAN** 1981 Strictly Private *edited by Roger McGough p.53*

© **SIMON DEWEY** 1995 (cover) Gold Dust *by Geraldine McCaughrean p.46*

© **SIMON DEWEY** 1994 (cover) Oliver Twist *by Charles Dickens p.59*

© **JANINA EDE** 1969 A Gift from Winklesea *by Helen Cresswell p.20*

© **CHARLOTTE FIRMIN** 1987 I'm Going on a Dragon Hunt *by Maurice Jones p.6*

© **CHRIS FISHER** 1994 Hedgehogs Don't Eat Hamburgers *by Vivian French & Chirs Fisher p.19*

© **MICHAEL FOREMAN** 1972 Dinosaurs and all That Rubbish *by Michael Foreman p.10*

© **MICHAEL FOREMAN** 1986 Early in the Morning *by Charles Causley p.24*

© **MICHAEL FOREMAN** 1983 Poems for 7-year-olds-and-under *edited by Helen Nicoll p.24*

© **MICHAEL FOREMAN** 1989 War Boy *by Michael Foreman p.34*

© **MICHAEL FOREMAN** Fairy Tales *by Terry Jones p.26*

© **MICHAEL FOREMAN/FREIRE WRIGHT** 1978 The Selfish Giant *by Oscar Wilde p.12*

© **ALISON FORSYTHE** 1995 (cover) The Friends *by Rosa Guy p.50*

© **SARAH GARLAND** 1990 Going to Playschool *by Sarah Garland p.4*

© **SARAH GARLAND** 1994 Pass it, Polly *by Sarah Garland p.26*

© **RUTH GERVIS** 1936 Ballet Shoes *by Noel Streatfeild p.43*

© **MAX GINSBURG** 1994 (cover) Roll of Thunder, Hear My Cry *by Mildred D Taylor p.52*

© **STANISLAV GLIWA** 1987 In Time of War *edited by Anne Harvey p.53*

© **EMILY HARE** 1995 (cover) Thirteen Something *by Jane Goldman p.53*

© **COLIN AND JACQUI HAWKINS** 1986 Max and the Magic Word *by Colin and Jacqui Hawkins p.6*

© **ERIC HILL** 1993 Spot's Walk in the Woods *by Eric Hill p.4*

© **ERIC HILL** 1994 Spot's Big Book of Colours, Shapes and Numbers *by Eric Hill p.14*

© **LILLIAN HOBAN** 1967 A Mouse and His Child *by Russell Hoban p.41*

© **BRUCE HOGARTH** 1993 The Bully *by Jan Needle p.42*

© **SALLY HOLMES** 1988 The Twig Thing *by Jan Mark p.21*

© **SHIRLEY HUGHES** 1977 It's too Frightening for Me *by Shirley Hughes p.21*

© **SHIRLEY HUGHES** 1984 Lucy and Tom's a.b.c *by Shirley Hughes p.14*

© **PAT HUTCHINS** 1971 Titch *by Pat Hutchins p.4*

© **PENNY IVES** 1993 Granny's Quilt *by Penny Ives p.10*

© **SUSAN JEFFERS** 1991 Brother Eagle, Sister Sky *by Chief Seattle & Susan Jeffers p.17*

© **RICHARD JONES** 1991 (cover) Along a Lonely Road *by Catherine Sefton p.42*

© **SALLY KILROY** 1990 Noah and the Rabbits *by Sally Kilroy p.2*

© **SATOSHI KITAMURA** 1993 Sky in the Pie *by Roger McGough p.33*

© **STEPHEN KING** 1994 (cover) Warriors *by Rupert Matthews p.25*

© **KATHRYN LAMB** 1993 Staying Cool Surviving School *by Rosie Rushton p.44*

© **ANTHONY LEWIS** 1994 Swim, Sam, Swim *by Leon Rosselson and Anthony Lewis p.19*

© **ALLAN MANHAM** 1985 (cover) Brother in the Land *by Robert Swindells p.51*

© **RON MARIS** 1983 My Book *by Ron Maris p.2*

© **JAMES MARSH** 1991 (cover) The Future-Telling Lady *by James Berry p.46*

© **SARA MIDDA** 1979 You Tell Me *by Roger McGough and Michael Rosen p.43*

© **SPIKE MILLIGAN** 1959 Silly Verse for Kids *by Spike Milligan p.43*

© **LEE MONTGOMERY** 1993 (cover) The Silver Sword *by Ian Serraillier p.43*

© **DAVID MOSTYN** 1985 Gargling with Jelly *by Brian Patten p.45*

© **CLAUDIO MUNOZ** 1991 This Little Puffin...edited *by Elizabeth Matterson p.5*

© **JILL MURPHY** 1974 The Worst Witch *by Jill Murphy p.23*

© **JILL MURPHY** 1995 The Worst Witch Spelling Book *by Jill Murphy & Rose Griffiths p.25*

© **RUSS NICHOLSON** 1982 The Warlock of Firetop Mountain *by Steve Jackson and Ian Livingstone p.44*

© **HILDA OFFEN** 1992 Nice Work, Little Wolf! *by Hilda Offen p.11*

© **HILDA OFFEN** 1990 Bella at the Ballet *by Brian Ball and Hilda Offen* p.19

© **JAN ORMEROD** 1982 Moonlight *by Jan Ormerod p.2*

© **DUNCAN PETERSEN PUBLISHING LTD** 1985 Creative Play *by Dorothy Einon p. 64*

© **JAN PIENKOWSKI** 1972 Meg and Mog *by Helen Nicoll p.5*

© **THE POINT** 1994 Talking Turkeys *by Benjamin Zephaniah p.53*

© **SUE PORTER** 1986 The Baked Bean Queen *by Rose Impey & Sue Porter p.10*

© **BEATRIX POTTER** 1902 The Tale of Peter Rabbit *by Beatrix Potter p.11*

© **MARY RAYNER** 1983 The Sheep-Pig *by Dick King-Smith p.31*

© **SHOO RAYNER** 1993 The Midnight Feast Joke Book *compiled by Shoo Rayner p.35*

© **CHRIS RIDDELL** 1994 Kasper in the Glitter *by Philip Ridley p.32*

© **JON RILEY** 1985 One Nil *by Tony Bradman p.20*

© **FRANK RODGERS** 1984 Mr Majeika *by Humphrey Carpenter p.22*

© **FRANK RODGERS** 1989 The Bunk-Bed Bus *by Frank Rodgers p.11*

© **MAUREEN ROFFEY** 1993 Ten Little Teddy Bears *by Maureen Roffey p.6*

© **TONY ROSS** 1978 Little Red Riding Hood retold *by Tony Ross p.13*

© **ALAN ROWE** 1990 Laughter is an Egg *by John Agard p.33*

© **JOHN RYAN** 1957 Captain Pugwash *by John Ryan p.14*

© **JOHN RYAN** 1984 Captain Pugwash and the Midnight Feast *by John Ryan p.21*

© **NICK SHARRATT** 1994 (cover) The Other Facts of Life *by Morris Gleitzman p.40*

© **POSY SIMMONDS** 1987 Fred *by Posy Simmonds p.12*

© **POSY SIMMONDS** 1981 Hot Dog and Other Poems *by Kit Wright p.33*

© **LANE SMITH** 1992 The Stinky Cheese Man and Other Fairly Stupid Tales *by Jon Scieszka and Lane Smith p.36*

© **ART SPIEGELMAN** Maus *by Art Spiegelman p.54*

©**PAUL STICKLAND** 1994 Dinosaur Roar! *by Paul and Henrietta Stickland p.5*

© **MIKE TERRY** 1994 (cover) Foxbusters *by Dick King-Smith p.57*

© **JULE VIVAS** 1984 Wilfrid Gordon McDonald Partridge *by Mem Fox p.10*

© **FRITZ WEGNER** 1980 Master Bun the Bakers' Boy *by Allan Ahlberg and Fritz Wegner* p.18

© **FRITZ WEGNER** 1986 Woof! *by Allan Ahlberg p.29*

© **GARTH WILLIAMS** 1952 Charlotte's Web *by E B White p.32*

© **SOPHY WILLIAMS** 1993 Moving *by Michael Rosen p.11*

© **BOB WILSON** 1983 Stanley Bagshaw and the Twenty Two Ton Whale *by Bob Wilson p.36*

50P OFF ANY PICTURE PUFFIN BOOK.
Available from all bookshops

CUSTOMER NAME _____

ADDRESS _____

_____ POSTCODE _____

CONDITIONS: All you have to do is take this voucher to any bookshop in the UK or Republic of Ireland before 31st January 1997 and present it at the counter with your purchase. *Don't forget to fill in your name and address on the voucher.*

This voucher cannot be exchanged for cash. Photocopies are not acceptable. Only one voucher can be used for any one purchase. This voucher can only be redeemed against a full priced Picture Puffin book and cannot be used in conjunction with any other price promotion. *Bookseller see reverse for details.*

--- ✂ ---

50P OFF ANY FIRST YOUNG PUFFIN.
Available from all bookshops

CUSTOMER NAME _____

ADDRESS _____

_____ POSTCODE _____

CONDITIONS: All you have to do is take this voucher to any bookshop in the UK or Republic of Ireland before 31st January 1997 and present it at the counter with your purchase. *Don't forget to fill in your name and address on the voucher.*

This voucher cannot be exchanged for cash. Photocopies are not acceptabl. Only one voucher can be used for any one purchase. This voucher can only be redeemed against a full priced First Young Puffin book and cannot be used in conjunction with any other price promotion. *Bookseller see reverse for details.*

--- ✂ ---

50P OFF ANY BOOK FROM THE HAPPY FAMILIES SERIES.
Available from all bookshops

CUSTOMER NAME _____

ADDRESS _____

_____ POSTCODE _____

CONDITIONS: All you have to do is take this voucher to any bookshop in the UK or Republic of Ireland before 31st January 1997 and present it at the counter with your purchase. *Don't forget to fill in your name and address on the voucher.*

This voucher cannot be exchanged for cash. Photocopies are not acceptabl. Only one voucher can be used for any one purchase. This voucher can only be redeemed against a full priced book in the Happy Families series and cannot be used in conjunction with any other price promotion. *Bookseller see reverse for details.*

Dear Bookseller,

Return this voucher to: PARENT'S GUIDE OFFER, PCS COMPUTING LTD, 80 BUCKINGHAM AVENUE, SLOUGH SL1 4PM.

Penguin will ensure, on presentation of this voucher, that you are refunded 50 pence for one Picture Puffin book sold using this voucher before 31st January 1997. *Note: **No voucher will be accepted after 28 February 1997.***

BOOKSHOP WHERE REDEEMED _____

ADDRESS _____

_____

_____

POSTCODE _____ **DATE** _____

Cash value 0.0001p

--✂

Dear Bookseller,

Return this voucher to: PARENT'S GUIDE OFFER, PCS COMPUTING LTD, 80 BUCKINGHAM AVENUE, SLOUGH SL1 4PM.

Penguin will ensure, on presentation of this voucher, that you are refunded 50 pence for one First Young Puffin book sold using this voucher before 31st January 1997. *Note: **No voucher will be accepted after 28 February 1997.***

BOOKSHOP WHERE REDEEMED _____

ADDRESS _____

_____

_____

POSTCODE _____ **DATE** _____

Cash value 0.0001p

--✂

Dear Bookseller,

Return this voucher to: PARENT'S GUIDE OFFER, PCS COMPUTING LTD, 80 BUCKINGHAM AVENUE, SLOUGH SL1 4PM.

Penguin will ensure, on presentation of this voucher, that you are refunded 50 pence for one Happy Families book sold using this voucher before 31st January 1997. *Note: **No voucher will be accepted after 28 February 1997.***

BOOKSHOP WHERE REDEEMED _____

ADDRESS _____

_____

_____

POSTCODE _____ **DATE** _____

Cash value 0.0001p

50p OFF ANY PUFFIN BOOK BY DICK KING-SMITH.
Available from all bookshops

CUSTOMER NAME _____

ADDRESS _____

_____ POSTCODE _____

CONDITIONS: All you have to do is take this voucher to any bookshop in the UK or Republic of Ireland before 31st January 1997 and present it at the counter with your purchase. *Don't forget to fill in your name and address on the voucher.*

This voucher cannot be exchanged for cash. Photocopies are not acceptable only one voucher can be used for any one purchase. This voucher can only be redeemed against a full priced Puffin book by Dick King-Smith and cannot be used in conjunction with any other price promotion. *Bookseller see reverse for details.*

50p OFF ANY PUFFIN BOOK BY PHILIP RIDLEY.
Available from all bookshops

CUSTOMER NAME _____

ADDRESS _____

_____ POSTCODE _____

CONDITIONS: All you have to do is take this voucher to any bookshop in the UK or Republic of Ireland before 31st January 1997 and present it at the counter with your purchase. *Don't forget to fill in your name and address on the voucher.*

This voucher cannot be exchanged for cash. Photocopies are not acceptable only one voucher can be used for any one purchase. This voucher can only be redeemed against a full priced Puffin book by Philip Ridley and cannot be used in conjunction with any other price promotion. *Bookseller see reverse for details.*

50p OFF ANY PUFFIN MODERN CLASSIC OR PUFFIN CLASSIC BOOK.
Available from all bookshops

CUSTOMER NAME _____

ADDRESS _____

_____ POSTCODE _____

CONDITIONS: All you have to do is take this voucher to any bookshop in the UK or Republic of Ireland before 31st January 1997 and present it at the counter with your purchase. *Don't forget to fill in your name and address on the voucher.*

This voucher cannot be exchanged for cash. Photocopies are not acceptable. Only one voucher can be used for any one purchase. This voucher can only be redeemed against a full priced Puffin Modern Classic or Puffin Classic book and cannot be used in conjunction with any other price promotion. *Bookseller see reverse for details.*

Dear Bookseller,

Return this voucher to: Parent's Guide Offer, PCS Computing Ltd, 80 Buckingham Avenue, Slough SL1 4PM.

Penguin will ensure, on presentation of this voucher, that you are refunded 50 pence for one Puffin book by Dick King-Smith sold using this voucher before 31st January 1997.
Note: No voucher will be accepted after 28 February 1997.

BOOKSHOP WHERE REDEEMED _____

ADDRESS _____

_____

_____

POSTCODE _____ **DATE** _____

Cash value 0.0001p

✂

Dear Bookseller,

Return this voucher to: Parent's Guide Offer, PCS Computing Ltd, 80 Buckingham Avenue, Slough SL1 4PM.

Penguin will ensure, on presentation of this voucher, that you are refunded 50 pence for one Puffin book by Philip Ridley sold using this voucher before 31st January 1997. *Note: No voucher will be accepted after 28 February 1997.*

BOOKSHOP WHERE REDEEMED _____

ADDRESS _____

_____

_____

POSTCODE _____ **DATE** _____

Cash value 0.0001p

✂

Dear Bookseller,

Return this voucher to: Parent's Guide Offer, PCS Computing Ltd, 80 Buckingham Avenue, Slough SL1 4PM.

Penguin will ensure, on presentation of this voucher, that you are refunded 50 pence for one Puffin Modern Classic or Puffin Classic book sold using this voucher before 31st January 1997.
Note: No voucher will be accepted after 28 February 1997.

BOOKSHOP WHERE REDEEMED _____

ADDRESS _____

_____

_____

POSTCODE _____ **DATE** _____

Cash value 0.0001p

2

DO YOU WANT MORE INFORMATION?

Puffin Books is part of Penguin Children's Books and has an extensive range of titles for children. Please fill in the form below for more information about children's books.
Send to: Parent's Guide Information, Puffin Books, 27 Wrights Lane, London W8 5TZ

NAME _____

ADDRESS _____

_____

_____

_____

NAME OF CHILD(REN)	**DATE OF BIRTH**	**SEX M/F**

RELATIONSHIP TO CHILD(REN) _____

COMMENTS ABOUT THE PARENT'S GUIDE _____

I would like more information regarding books published by Penguin and
Puffin Books *(please tick)*

☐ A complete list of Penguin Children's Books

☐ Books suitable for the National Curriculum for England and Wales

☐ Books for Reluctant Readers

☐ Books for Gifted Readers

☐ I do not wish for any of my comments about the Parent's Guide to be used on promotional material

☐ I would not like to receive additional information about Penguin Children's Books

Return your questionnaire to:
Parent's Guide Information,
Puffin Books,
27 Wrights Lane,
London W8 5TZ

You will be sent the information requested within 28 days.